The Miracle Museum

Where Veterans' Hearts Find Healing

By Lee Grimes

As told to
Julie McDonald Zander

Copyright © 2014

Lee Grimes of the Veterans Memorial Museum

and Julie McDonald Zander of Chapters of Life

No part of this publication may be reproduced or transmitted in any form or by any means, electronic or mechanical, including photocopy, recording, or any information storage or retrieval system, without permission in writing from the authors.

ISBN 978-1-939685-16-2

Designed and edited by Julie McDonald Zander
Chapters of Life
Toledo, Washington
www.chaptersoflife.com

Proofreading by Sue Miholer of Picky, Picky Ink in Keizer, Oregon

Cover design by April Prestegord

Dedication

This book is dedicated to all the men and women
who have served in the armed forces,
in war and in peacetime,
to provide and protect the God-given freedom
that America has always enjoyed.
May we, the recipients of that freedom,
always remember, honor and uphold the sacrifices
made by each and every one of these brave men and women.
Without their military service,
America would not be what it is today,
the greatest nation on the face of the earth!

Contents

Preface

The Miracle Museum is the story of how the Veterans Memorial Museum was spiritually inspired. As a result of the Fourth of July Patriotic Programs at the Centralia First Church of God, the founder of the museum was visited by the Holy Spirit and given the following message:

"No, don't let them forget; go out and get their stories."

From the spiritual encounter that night, the Veterans Memorial Museum was born and has flourished under God's guidance. This book relates the many miracles that unfolded as the museum grew from an idea to the worldwide recognized memorial it is today.

After touring the museum, many people have asked, "How did this get started?" or "How can such a beautiful facility be maintained in such a small town?" or "What was the inspiration to build such a memorial?" The answers are provided within the following pages.

The Miracle Museum is based on the recollections of the author of the events and conversations as they unfolded during the first sixteen years of the Veterans Memorial Museum. The quotes are as close to verbatim as remembered, but may not be exact. When at all possible, the stories related in this book were verified by the subject.

Lee T. Grimes

Years ago, Lee Grimes told me about hearing a voice in the wee hours of the morning telling him to make sure veterans' stories aren't forgotten. I've always figured God needed to whack me with a sledgehammer so I could hear His voice.

A decade later, corresponding by email with Lee to organize a personal historians' meeting at the museum, he mentioned my work helping the museum publicize its events. I responded in an email that I hadn't done much, but said someday I'd love to help him share the story of how the museum began. But, before I sent the email, I erased that statement, believing it was too presumptuous to suggest such a thing. Lee responded by email, again thanking me for what I had done … and then said he hoped I would help him tell the story of *The Miracle Museum*. The sledgehammer! I wrote back immediately and explained that I had just erased that line from my previous email. Praise the Lord!

I felt honored to meet with Lee eight times to capture stories about the birth and growth of the museum. I tapped furiously at the keyboard as Lee shared stories about veterans who experienced healing inside the museum. During each interview, goosebumps prickled my arms and tears sprang to my eyes as I heard how God has worked in the lives of so many people, healing decades-old wounds and bringing peace to war-ravaged hearts.

Thank you, Lee, for heeding that still, small voice, and for helping me hear it too.

Julie McDonald Zander

ACKNOWLEDGMENTS

This book could not have been written without the inspiration, guidance, and support of the following:

God—Through His infinite knowledge, He chose this book, this author, and this museum as a venue to honor and remember the service and sacrifices of our veterans.

Veterans—Without the veterans who served so valiantly to protect our nation and our freedom, we would have no museum to preserve and honor their sacrifices. Without the veterans sharing their most personal stories, fears, and tears, there would be no book to write.

Julie McDonald Zander—Without Julie's literary knowledge and guidance through the research, drafting, and edits, this book would not have been accomplished. Julie laughed and cried as we worked our way through the pages. She always encouraged me to take the next step.

Barbara Grimes—My wife, Barb, is the love of my life. She has encouraged me in all my endeavors our entire marriage. From the first morning I told her of my spiritual visitation, she has been by my side with encouragement and love, never saying a discouraging word. When I got tired in the early morning hours as I pondered over the pages, she would always say "I am proud of you." Without Barb, this book would never have made it to print.

Family and friends—My many family members and friends who encouraged me to continue writing the book. Their support has always lifted me up and given me strength.

Introduction

The call to pay tribute to the men and women who have served, are serving, and will serve was given to Lee Grimes early one morning many years ago.

The story of how what started as an idea, inspired during annual Fourth of July services at a church, later became a museum dedicated to remembering veterans is told within the pages of this book.

As Lee set out to tell the story, as only he could, he ventured back in time to:

- the wake-up call from God
- interviewing the veterans
- collecting memorabilia
- finding the building
- opening the first museum building in Centralia
- growth
- finding property and support from the city of Chehalis
- plans for new building
- finding the finances

The items above are all critical; many told us impossible. However, through all of history, when God gives the direction, He also provides the way. People from all over the country—veterans and non-veterans—stepped forward to share the dream.

The purpose of this book is to honor the veterans who have given, since the formation of this country, a portion of their lives or provided the ultimate sacrifice—their lives—so we can continue to enjoy the freedoms this country has provided since its inception. It has been said many times that FREEDOM IS NOT FREE, but how many people really understand the price these veterans pay?

This book will not tell the story of every veteran who has ever served, or even every veteran whose story is showcased at the museum. Instead, it tells individual stories about real veterans with their specific stories that allow each of us a rare glimpse into a part of their service.

Some parts of the stories on the pages that follow share a common thread: duty to country and the bond developed with brothers and sisters in arms. This has always been true of those who serve in combat and those who provide the support. As one combat veteran once said, "Those of us in combat areas are like the quarterback on a football team; if you took all the other players away, there is no possibility any plans could succeed."

You, or people you know, may wonder why anyone would want to join the military. These pages tell you why from the only group qualified to answer that question—those who made that choice. Many times I have been overwhelmed by their stories and absolutely humbled when I absorb the fact that the great majority of these people were teenagers or in their early twenties.

As Lee edited these pages, we shared the memories and acknowledged that we are so grateful to leave as our legacy a museum that honors those who gave so much. The veterans opened their circle and allowed us in: We are now and always will be humbly grateful.

As the museum is not a war museum, this book is not a war book. It is a story of people with a purpose—freedom. You will at times experience sadness, wonderment, laughter. What are you waiting for? Turn the page to begin the journey.

Written with the utmost of respect and love for my husband and his obedience to God's call, and for all the veterans and their families we have been blessed to know ~

Barb Grimes
Co-Founder

The Miracle Museum

Where Veterans' Hearts Find Healing

Chapter One:

FROM A MIRACLE TO A MUSEUM

A HALF DOZEN MEN IN ARMY COMBAT FATIGUES raced down the aisles, pivoting with guns pointed, gunfire blasting over the sound system as they spied unseen enemies in the dimly lit church.

The men dove behind a makeshift foxhole fashioned from sandbags as smoke bombs obscured the podium while the audience watched the drama unfold.

The scene, re-created at the Centralia First Church of God to depict what veterans faced on the battlefront in Vietnam, was designed to honor the sacrifices of military men and women who have served the United States of America.

It was all part of the annual Fourth of July Patriotic Program, which is one reason my wife, Barbara, and I began attending this Southwest Washington church in the late 1980s. We loved participating in these skits.

After the skit ended, worship leader Dallas Fast led hundreds of people in songs honoring the United States of America and its military. We'd ask a veteran from each branch of the service to carry a flag to the front, where they'd stand on the podium while the choir sang each branch's anthem.

Then the Rev. Darcy Fast invited all military veterans to the podium.

The 2000 color guard for the Patriotic Program, from left, Jack Williams, USMC; Dale Ingle, USA; Terry Lowery, USN; George Kelder, USCG; C.J. Fox, USAF; Roger Flinn, USMC; Pat Swanson, USA; and in front Lee Grimes.

Barb and I watched Vietnam Army veteran Pat Swanson walk to the front of the church, wearing his 1st Air Cavalry Division Army uniform. I had encouraged him to wear it and even enlisted the help of his wife. He said he'd rather forget those years in combat.

As greeters at the door, I shook Pat's hand and Barb shed tears.

"You look wonderful," I said. His wife, Sherry, told me she put the uniform on the end of the bed that morning and asked him again to wear it. He finally relented.

I watched with immense pride as the military men and women stood before the congregation. The church reverberated with the applause of hundreds who gave the veterans a fifteen-minute standing ovation.

After the program ended, Pat Swanson walked over to me.

"When I was standing on the podium with the rest of the veterans, it was like I was the only one

Vietnam veteran Pat Swanson wearing his Army uniform after nearly thirty years.

there," he said. "I felt it come from the bottom of my feet, through the top of my head. That was my welcome home. That was my healing that day."

That's when I realized that what we were doing in the church was good. I began to realize how much our veterans hurt inside. Those of us who were never there, we have empathy for them but cannot feel what's inside their hearts and minds.

That's where seeds for the Veterans Memorial Museum were planted.

Our patriotic programs also grew, drawing 1,500 people on Saturday nights and Sunday mornings each year. Sometimes we showed videos of military life.

Barb and I started going to garage sales, antique stores, and military shows; we'd buy old uniforms, helmets, documents, and other unusual items. By the early 1990s, we filled that entire church foyer with military items. We asked veterans to wear their uniforms and sit beside their displays.

Norman Willard, a World War I veteran who was nearly a hundred years old, sat beside his display in his suit. His pants crawled up, showing his legs. I mentioned that fact to him.

"I'm showing off my leg for all the girls around here," he responded with his wonderful sense of humor.

WWI veteran Norman Willard with his display at Centralia First Church of God in 1997.

Whenever Barb and I met military veterans, we invited them to the patriotic program.

Along with our friend Loren Estep, Barb and I played polkas, waltzes, and other numbers at nursing homes, dances, and other events. Barb played the accordion, Loren the banjo, and I the tuba. We called ourselves the Polka Dots.

"The Polka Dots" Lee Grimes, tuba, Barb Grimes, accordion, and Loren Estep, banjo.

We often invited people to join us, and Ed Redinger, a World War II Navy veteran, would play guitar. Sometimes when we would play in a difficult key, he'd stomp off the stage in an angry fit. That's just the way he was.

I respected Ed as a veteran, and in the summer of 1993, I invited him to one of our Fourth of July celebrations. Lo and behold, he showed up.

Once again, we invited veterans to the podium, where they were recognized with applause. Ed stood there with the Navy guys.

After the program, Barb and I lingered, chatting with Dallas Fast. Ed walked up to us.

"This is the most wonderful program I have ever seen to honor veterans," he said.

Then tears streamed down his cheeks as he whispered in a choked voice, "You know, we are the forgotten ones."

Then he turned and walked away.

Those were probably the most important words ever spoken to me. The impact they made struck deep into my heart.

Is that how veterans feel? The church had produced this program for years to honor veterans, and I couldn't help thinking, *Don't they realize there are people out there who remember and honor them?*

The more I thought about it, the more I realized, except for that one day a year at church, and perhaps on Veterans Day or Memorial Day, nobody knows who they are or what they have done.

I couldn't shake those words. I began to see people differently. I would ask men and women I met, "Are you a veteran?"

God had planted a seed and watered it.

Awakening in the Night

I'm a sound sleeper and a slow getter-upper. I have always been able to sleep deeply through the night, never awakening.

But in the fall of 1994, I woke from a dead sleep. I looked at the clock on the bedstead: 3 a.m. Then I felt a presence about me. My body shivered with chills, my hair felt like it was standing up on the back of my neck. I had experienced a similar feeling once or twice before in my life, but never as forcefully.

I felt strongly, *This is not a dream. It's real.*

Then I heard these words clearly in my mind: "No, don't let them forget. Go out and get their stories."

That was it. Then it was gone.

I lay there quietly. I didn't wake Barb, but I knew what had happened. God had sent the Holy Spirit or an angel to give me a message. Only when we meet face to face can He tell me how the message was delivered. But it was delivered. I knew I needed to interview veterans to hear their stories.

I didn't sleep the rest of the night. I knew I had just experienced a spiritual encounter. I felt full of joy. I felt humbled. Why would God visit me? Who am I?

Although I had given my heart fully to the Lord, I had never experienced such a powerful spiritual visitation. I saw smaller miracles, but nothing so dramatic and fulfilling.

Barb woke up at five that morning.

"Honey," I said. "God spoke to me last night."

"What did He say?"

"'Don't let them forget. Go out and get their stories.' So, what am I going to do?"

She didn't hesitate.

"You're going to go out and start interviewing veterans," Barb said.

I didn't have a video camera. She told me to buy one. I bought one that day. I typed a couple of pages of basic questions to ask veterans: When did you join the service? Where did you go to boot camp? How did it feel to leave the family? How did you feel in the combat zone? Were you afraid? Did you have God in your heart? Did you pray before you left? Are you proud of your service? Would you do it again?

I always explained that we were recording their stories for historical purposes, for their family members, for their great-great-grandchildren who would want to hear about their service to their country in their own words.

I always ended the same way: "Is there something you would like to leave for future generations?"

Probably 95 percent of them said, "If you ever have the opportunity to serve your country, do it."

INTERVIEWING VETERANS

The first person I interviewed was Loren Estep, my sister-in-law's uncle by marriage. His nephew, Don Roberts, had married Barb's sister, Arlene.

I thought he'd be easy to interview because he was family. We knew him well. Explaining that I was starting a new project interviewing veterans, I asked if he would be my first one.

"Nobody's ever sat down and asked me about my Navy time before," Loren said.

I drove to his house, bringing an American flag with me. He dug out his uniform and a few other items of memorabilia. We set the uniform on one side and the flag on the other, with a blue sheet for a backdrop.

I began asking him a few questions, and by golly, it didn't take long before he just started relating his story. It took very little prompting.

We had no idea what Loren had gone through. He served as an electrician in the Pacific on one of the heavier combat vessels, the USS

Steamer Bay CVE-87, an aircraft carrier made in Vancouver, Washington, and commissioned in April 1944.

He saw the deck of another aircraft carrier burst into flames after a kamikaze pilot crashed and fiery pieces of wood falling into the water. Later, a psychologist helped him admit that it wasn't wood falling into the water—it was men. That was something Loren had tried to block.

Another time, with the *Steamer Bay* behind another carrier in a convoy, the order came to switch positions. They switched, and a kamikaze pilot hit the carrier behind the *Steamer Bay*. It would have been his ship if they had not switched places.

He also talked about his service as a Merchant Marine during the Korean War.

When we finished the interview, he said, "This was pretty neat. I have a friend you need to talk to."

He introduced me to Spencer Strasser from Napavine, who had served in U.S. Army Gen. George Patton's tank force in Europe during WWII. I interviewed him with the same blue backdrop, a flag on one side, his uniform on the other. He brought out his medals and I zoomed in on them.

He told me about being in the tank corps. He was in the third tank in a column, and as they rolled into this shot-up German village, two young men darted across the street into a demolished building. His tank kept rolling. Suddenly, two bazooka rounds fired from inside the building struck the tank, killing two men. Strasser took shrapnel in his body and spent several months in the hospital, where they inserted metal plates into his head.

"Maybe that's what's wrong with me today," he told me. It's interesting how they find humor in such horrific experiences.

The infantry killed the two young Hitler youths.

Spencer gave me the names of a few more veterans. That's how the interviews progressed, from one veteran to another. Although I was working full time in a cabinet shop, I conducted about sixty interviews during a year, primarily in the evenings and on weekends.

Most interviews lasted two or three hours. Sometimes the veteran would go off in a different direction, which was fine.

I began to see immediately the relief that a lot of these veterans experienced as they shared their stories.

Then Pastor Jack Marshall of the Salkum Community Church, who lived on Middle Fork Road outside Chehalis, asked if I'd like to interview one of the last remaining WWI veterans.

Norman Willard, the WWI veteran who enjoyed showing his legs to girls, was ninety-nine years and nine months old when I interviewed him. He lived behind Steck Clinic at Woodland Estates Retirement Center in Chehalis, so after church on a Sunday afternoon, I packed my gear. Accompanied by Pastor Marshall and his wife, Denise, I braced myself to see a hundred-year-old man, wondering how I'd handle the interview. I never should have doubted.

When we knocked on the door, we heard a robust, "Come on in!" Norm looked no more than eighty years old, a tall, good-looking gentleman sitting in a chair, just as spry as could be. His little mite of a wife was there, too.

I set up and switched on the equipment and started asking questions.

Norm, who had a very good memory for details, was born September 16, 1895, on State Street in Chehalis. Norm left Chehalis on the local train and traveled to Camp Lewis where he was inducted into the Army. After Army boot camp, he was sent to New York and embarked on a ship overseas, serving in the 42nd Infantry Division. He played baseball in France on an Army exhibition team, an activity that helped raise troop morale.

One night, while Norm was reading in bed by candlelight, an old sergeant staggered in "drunker than a skunk."

Seeing the candle, the sergeant bragged, "I bet I can shoot that light out over old Willard's head." Norm looked up, saw the guy waving his rifle around, and kablooey—he shot the candle. Norm said that's as close to death as he ever came.

In France, Norm traveled to the trenches in wagons, bringing ammunition and sometimes returning with German prisoners. One time, on the way back to the compound, he and another guy cut through a rail yard and found an open rail car filled with Karo syrup. The men all craved sugar, which was in great shortage, so they each grabbed a tin can, plunged their bayonet into it, and proceeded to drink the syrup.

Norm talked about a close friend of his in the trenches. "You, being a Christian, will understand this story," he told me.

"In the trenches there are areas called the 'active sectors' where a lot of the heavy fighting is going on. Then there are the 'quiet sectors' where very little action is taking place. Many times reserves are pulled from the quiet sector. Quietly and unknown to the Americans, the Germans had amassed a large force in front of the quiet sector. As the Germans charged his position, the friend heard loud shouting and the pounding of thousands of horses' hooves behind him. The Germans stopped the attack and retreated. Standing, his friend looked all around: Not a horse in sight.

"What do you think it was?" Norm asked me.

"Legions of angels," I replied.

As it's been with many soldiers throughout history, Norm thought the native girls looked pretty good. As a tall, handsome young man, he found a French girl who admired him too. On one of his days of leave, Norm was invited to the girl's home to meet her parents. Norm thought he would impress her parents by learning some French. He studied a little manual given to all the soldiers and, when he was introduced to her parents, he intended to say, "I have traveled across this beautiful field of flowers to come to your home." However, what came out in the translation was, "I have traveled across this beautiful field of manure to come to your home!" Despite a couple of raised eyebrows, Norm was invited in. He never saw the girl again after the war.

On Armistice Day, November 11, 1918, Norm was in Paris, where grateful French people danced in the streets and treated American soldiers to free liquor and food.

After finishing the interview, Norm said when he returned from the war, he joined the WWI Veterans Association. "There would just be a sea of us veterans," he said.

But in the 1980s, serving as a state officer, he attended his last meeting. Standing at the lectern, he saw only a handful of men. As he looked out, he told me he wondered, *Who's going to remember us when we're gone?*

After the interview, Norm's question lingered in my mind. A lot of the WWII veterans I interviewed voiced the same question.

One weekend, before our musical group performed at the Music Factory, a Christian music hall in Elma, Washington, I remember talking to a Korean War veteran on the street. He looked down, kicking rocks with his foot, and muttered, "You know, we fought a forgotten war." He didn't want to look up. It was sad.

I interviewed three or four Vietnam veterans, too. They'd just as soon forget their war.

A Place to Remember Veterans

I began to see a common theme. It didn't make any difference in what war these veterans fought. What mattered to them is that people remember their service after they're gone. Would their uniforms and medals be tucked away in a dusty old trunk, tossed away after they died?

These stories were important. They told the story not just of individuals, but of America and why we're here.

A lot of people don't realize these veterans carry real pain with them. They don't share it, but keep it inside. Although through the years they had shared bits and pieces, they had seldom told their story in detail until I conducted these interviews.

Many wept as they released the pain, telling their stories to a non-veteran, somebody who technically doesn't understand what they went through. I often wondered, *Why are they telling me?* But I knew. God prepared the way, giving these people the comfort to know that I genuinely cared about what they had endured.

Many pulled their uniforms from old trunks, asking if I wanted them. I accepted items for the church program. We filled the guest bedroom with boxes of memorabilia and racks of uniforms. Then we filled the garage; we could scarcely park in it. Then we put items in the living room. When they encroached on the television, Barb said, "That's enough."

I had interviewed veterans for a year, collecting their incredible stories and gathering artifacts, or props, that enhanced the stories. Although a lot of collectors place emphasis on the items, the story is the most important thing.

I told Barb I had been thinking for some time that we should start a museum to honor our veterans, with the stories as the focus.

"If you think God's leading you there, then I'm with you," she said.

In late 1995, we visited Laurel Tiller, a Centralia attorney, and told him we wanted to start a museum but didn't know how to begin. He said we first needed a five- or seven-member board of directors. Then we needed to file Articles of Incorporation with the Secretary of State, draft bylaws, and obtain an IRS designation as a 501(c)3 nonprofit.

First board of directors meeting, in front, Les Dooley and Loren Estep; back, Lee Grimes, Patti Estep, and Jeffrey Grimes.

We selected five members to form a board of directors: Loren and Patti Estep; my son, Jeffrey Grimes, a Navy veteran from Napavine, Washington; Les Dooley of Centralia, a Marine lance corporal who served in WWII; and me. We filed Articles of Incorporation, but learned that no more than 40 percent of the board could be relatives. Patti agreed to step down, and we invited WWII Navy Pearl Harbor survivor G.A. "Cy" Simmons of Adna, Washington, to serve as a board member. He agreed.

All were veterans except me. We filed the paperwork and chartered the museum on December 5, 1995.

Then we began looking for a building in Centralia or Chehalis. But we had no money.

During 1996, I visited branches of the Veterans of Foreign Wars and American Legion, seeking support for the museum. At service organizations, I shared our dream of creating a museum to honor veterans. I asked if they could help. We sold museum memberships for twenty dollars each. Slowly we gathered a bit of money.

When Norman Willard discovered our plans to build a museum for veterans, he insisted on donating the first dollar. We turned down his money

Norm Willard presenting the museum with its first "seed dollar" donation.

until we obtained our IRS 501c3 nonprofit status. When we did, this proud WWI veteran dressed in a suit and donated that first dollar as seed money. We gave all local WWI veterans an honorary membership.

We also gave an honorary membership to Army Spc. 4th Class Thomas James Kinsman of Onalaska, Washington, recipient of the military's highest award, the Medal of Honor. He earned the medal as a private by throwing himself on a grenade in Vietnam to save seven fellow Army infantrymen.

We kept searching for a place to locate the museum, and finally found the old War-Mur Electric & Telephone building at 712 W. Main St. in Centralia, which was available for rent after junk dealers had moved out. Charlie Ward, a WWII Army Air Force veteran, owned the 3,500-square-foot building. The cost was $950 a month, regardless of business type.

Barb and I asked Loren and Patti Estep if they'd co-found the museum with us, sharing the expense of the monthly rent until the museum could financially cover the costs. They agreed, so the Grimes and the Esteps each paid $475 a month for the rent as a gift to the museum. Later, the museum paid forty dollars toward the rent, increasing its share by forty dollars each month until it covered the entire payment within two years.

We took possession of the building in April 1997. We needed to renovate the building, but the landlord didn't want to pay for it and we didn't have the money. We asked bank officials if the museum could obtain a loan; the answer was no. We needed to put up personal collateral to guarantee the loan.

So Barb and I stepped out in faith once again.

Loren and Patti Estep, co-founders of the Veterans Memorial Museum, 1997.

I started collecting baseball cards when I was nine. In high school, my interest waned, but at thirty, I resumed my hobby, attending shows and buying the cards I wanted. When we bought our house a decade later, we owed $75,000. We needed money to pay off the mortgage, so I sold perhaps 30,000 baseball cards to help pay off the loan.

By 1996, we had just paid off our house. For the first time ever, we didn't have a mortgage, a goal we had worked all our lives to achieve.

But to renovate the museum, we offered our house as collateral to borrow $40,000.

"God's leading us this way," Barb reasoned. "No problem. It's going to take care of itself."

To Barb, there is no gray area. But I tend to worry. I knew we weren't going to lose the house. What is the worst that could happen? We'd have to pay back $40,000. I knew the house was worth a lot more than that.

The bank approved the loan in April, and work began immediately. From April until November, two dozen volunteers yanked out walls, repaired ceilings, replaced the toilets, remodeled and enlarged the bathroom, fixed the chimney, painted walls, and installed carpeting.

The $40,000 covered materials: paint, carpeting, glass for cabinets, and wood.

I still worked full time at the cabinet shop. After work each day, I would stop at the museum, laboring until one in the morning. Sometimes I stayed after hours at the shop, carefully creating the museum's display

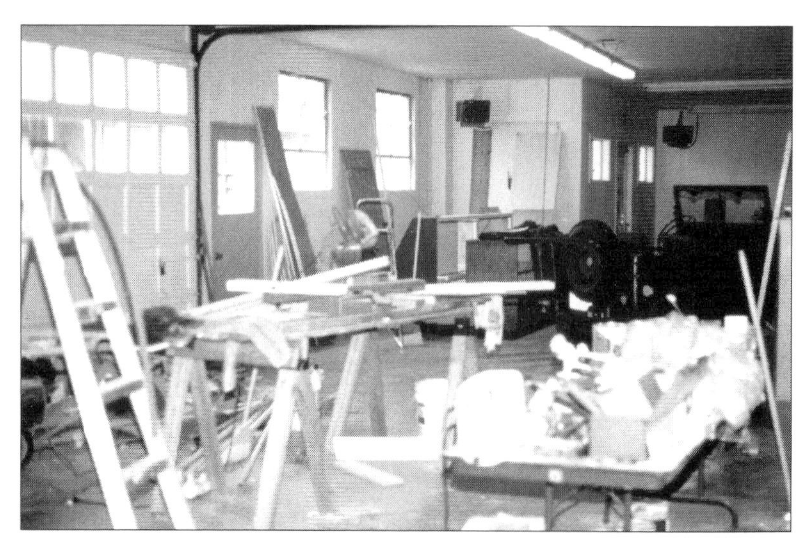

In May 1997, renovation of the interior of the building has started, above; at left, Loren Estep, left, and Ed Weed tore down the old defunct chimney; and below, Allen Grimes assists me with spraying directional arrows on the floor.

cabinets. After three or four hours of sleep, I'd return to work.

I always prayed that God would keep me lifted up. He did!

The final night before the grand opening, my brother, Allen Grimes, helped me spray the floor traffic directional arrows. Allen had served as a helicopter mechanic in the Army from 1956 through 1959 and had been stationed in Korea for eighteen months. I have always highly respected Allen for his military service. I wanted to be just like my big brother and join the Army. I remember dressing in Allen's Army uniform at the ripe old age of eleven, ready to fight for my country like my big brother.

Lee Grimes, age eleven, wearing his brother Allen Grimes' Army uniform when Allen was home on furlough.

Allen and his wife, Patsy, had traveled nearly 1,300 miles from South Dakota to be here for the grand opening. I believe they traveled the farthest to help us celebrate this memorable day. To have Allen help me put the final touches on the museum has always been very special.

Opening the Museum

The museum opened on Veterans Day, November 11, 1997, to great fanfare. Our grand opening ceremony took place in Washington Park. I addressed the audience of nearly four hundred, sharing what we were doing to honor our veterans with a museum.

Pat Swanson served as master of ceremonies, Army Vietnam veteran Johnny Dunnagan sang "A Hero for Today," the Rev. Darcy Fast gave the invocation, and Pastor Dallas Fast led the crowd in singing "God Bless America."

A veteran representing each war spoke about what the museum meant to them. They were Dave Bussard, who served in the Army Air Corps during WWII; Ron Harmon, a Marine in the Korean War who also served three tours in Vietnam; Ken Rollins, an Army soldier in Vietnam; and Frank Handoe, an Army veteran from the Persian Gulf War.

At the end of the program, Pat called all veterans in the audience to attention. He asked Barb and me to step forward. Then he commanded everyone to present arms.

Hand salute given to Lee and Barb Grimes during the grand opening ceremony November 11, 1997.

Seeing these veterans saluting us overwhelmed me. Here these people who had done so much to serve this country were saluting us. It should have been the other way around. But I knew why they were doing it, because we were honoring them. Barb and I both cried.

We then walked several blocks west on Main Street to the storefront museum, where Cy Simmons had erected a flagpole. The Civil Air Patrol ran our first flag up during the ceremony. Then we cut the ribbon on the front door and invited people inside.

Across the street, a reader board at Papa Ray's restaurant stated, "Thank you, Lee and Barb, from Veterans."

The crowd stood shoulder to shoulder in the small building, and a line snaked around the corner as others waited to enter and view the sixty display cases inside.

Admission was $3 for adults, $1.50 for students, and free to museum members. Annual membership dues were twenty dollars for veter-

Cy Simmons "running up the colors" on the Navy-style mast flagpole he designed and donated.

ans and seniors, twenty-five for other adults, ten for students, forty for families, and fifty for organizations and businesses.

It was incredible and heartwarming. Everyone was so thrilled with what they saw.

Display cases were filled with Revolutionary War military items; canteens, bugles, and an 1864 cavalry saber from the Civil War; a musician's tunic from the Spanish-American War; and the drum pounded by American Legionnaires during that first fateful Armistice Day Parade in Centralia November 11, 1919, when violence erupted, leaving four Legionnaires dead and a lynch mob storming the city jail to kill a member of the Industrial Woodworkers of the World, or Wobblies.

Other cases featured Norm Willard's uniform from WWI, as well as a trench periscope and Navy hammock from that war; a pigeon cage with parachute used to send messages in Europe during WWII, a mine detector kit, and K rations; a bazooka anti-tank gun used during the Korean War, as well as assault weapons, rations, and black, heavy cold weather footwear referred to as Mickey Mouse boots. Other cases showed the uniforms, guns, and memorabilia from the veterans of the wars in Vietnam and the Persian Gulf.

Memories surfaced as veterans sipped coffee, nibbled cake, and swapped stories. We accepted memberships and made everyone who came to the museum that day a charter member. We have 141 charter members.

During its first seven months, the museum was open only three days a week. Nearly 1,500 visitors came through the doors the first year. During 1999, more than 250 people visited the museum each month, twice as many as the previous year.

Through donations, memberships, T-shirt sales, and admissions, the museum repaid its loan to Lee and Barb within three years.

A Poem to Remember

Shortly before we opened the museum in Centralia, God inspired me to write a poem.

I had interviewed quite a few veterans by 1996 and, watching television one night while sitting in my recliner, I suddenly felt as if God shook me up and told me to grab a piece of paper and write this down.

So I did. It took twenty minutes to write what flowed through my mind. Other than correcting a few spelling errors, I left it the way I wrote it that day.

We printed the poem on the back of all our membership applications. The poem has touched so many people when I recite it, which I've done in Seattle, Portland, Yakima, Ocean Shores, and countless other places.

Sometimes when I introduce myself, people respond to me by saying, "Lee Grimes? Are you the guy who wrote the poem?"

I've received many requests from organizations to reprint the poem. I always agree, as long as nobody profits financially from it. One of the veterans told me I need to copyright it, which I did.

As I interviewed these veterans, I learned so much from them. But I also discovered one common refrain: Who will remember when we're gone? Whether they served in WWI or Korea, WWII or Vietnam, the vets I've interviewed always wonder, "Who's going to remember when I'm gone?"

The poem is titled, "Who Will Remember?"

WHO WILL REMEMBER?

Who will remember the Great World War, the trenches, the wire and the gas? Who will remember those long ago places our brave young men were at?

Who will remember places named the Marne, St. Mihiel, Norroy, Chateau-Thierry, Belleau Wood, and the deadly Meuse-Argonne? Vittorio-

Veneto, Colmar, Aisne and the Somme. Who will remember these? Will it be only those who were there?

Who will remember World War II and all the battles fought? Who will remember the ships and planes and the glory that they brought?

Arizona, South Dakota, Nicholas, Ommaney Bay; Lexington, Shannon, Sea Wolf and lucky Steamer Bay. Memphis Belle, Skirty Bert, Barbie, Punkie II; Lady Luck, Shoo Shoo Baby and Carolina Moon. Who will remember these? Will it be only those who were there?

Kilay Ridge, Aka Shima, Tarawa, Camp O'Donnell; Funifuti, Bataan, Iwo Jima and Okinawa. Casablanca, Mareth Line, Bizerte, Hill 609; D-Day, Cherbourg, the Bulge, and the crossing of the Rhine. Who will remember these? Will it be only those who were there?

Who will remember the Korean War, those cold frostbitten feet?
Who will remember the battles fought in the valleys and on the peaks?

Pusan, Inchon, Naktong, The Bean Patch; Kimpo Field, Chosin Reservoir and the Toktong Pass. Yalu River, Punch Bowl, Hamhung, Hill 342; 38th Parallel, Seoul, Line of Demarcation.
Who will remember these? Will it only be those who were there?

Who will remember the Vietnam War, fought for so many years?
Young men died and women cried and at home there were no cheers.

Pleiku, Parrot's Beak, Da Nang, Phu Bai; Ben Het, Fishhook, The Tet and Chu Lai. Khe Sanh, Mekong, DMZ, Cam Ranh Bay; Rockpile, Tunnel Rats, Hamburger Hill and Hue. Who will remember these? Will it only be those who were there?

Who will remember the Persian Gulf War, fought on distant desert sand? Who will remember what went on to stop incursion once again?

Suez Canal, Kuwait City, Baghdad, the sand of Iraq; Desert Shield, Desert Storm and Scud missile attacks. Basra, Euphrates River, Haifa, Tel

Aviv; Republican Guard, Dharan and Stealth bomber raids. Who will remember these? Will it be only those who were there?

Who will remember our undeclared wars, the ones that kept evil at bay? Who will remember our peace time forces, ready to pay their way?

Who will remember Bay of Pigs, the Cold War, Grenada, Somalia? Who will remember Haiti, Panama City, and now Bosnia?

Who will remember? Will it be only those who were there?

© Lee T. Grimes 1996
All Rights Reserved

I used to write a little verse in high school and sweet little things to my wife when we first married. But God wrote this poem and I penned it.

Sometimes people ask me, "How do you know God inspired you to write that?"

You just know. If you're a Christian, you know. If I had said, "To heck with it," it would have slipped away.

The names and places in the poem were those I heard from veterans I interviewed. Sometimes veterans speak to me afterward, saying, "I was there." Occasionally, a guy will say to me, "Well, you didn't say anything about where I was … or my battle." But when they say that, they have missed the point of the poem. It's not just those few specific battles; it shows the vastness of where all our veterans have served and the sacrifices that have been made. This poem is inclusive of all who have ever served this great nation in the armed forces.

My dream is to someday recite this poem on the steps of the Capitol Building in Washington, D.C., perhaps at a Veterans Day program.

When I recite it at presentations, I explain that this is the reason we built the Veterans Memorial Museum, first in Centralia and then in Chehalis, where gold lettering on a sign on the front of the large building promises: "They Shall Not Be Forgotten."

Chapter Two:

Healing Veterans' Wounded Hearts

THE FIRST EVENT WE HELD AT THE MUSEUM was a party celebrating Norman Willard's one hundredth birthday. We hadn't even officially opened the museum. The gallery was empty, but Norm and his wife arrived, along with friends, family members, museum volunteers, and board members. Norm passed away August 15, 1998.

Before we opened the museum, as we were setting up displays, a gentleman entered the building. Buck Winterowd, a man in his seventies, told me he still had a lot of items from his war days. He asked if we wanted it. During WWII, he had served with U.S. Army Gen. George Patton's tank corps in North Africa. He brought in medals, uniforms, photographs, memorabilia, and a pair of dice. I asked him about the dice.

"You don't know how many games of craps I've won and lost on blankets in North Africa with those dice," he said.

He showed me a ring crafted by a Moroccan, a German ammo box that he covered with blue and adorned with upholstery buttons, and a pocket watch, the glass cracked and hands missing.

The watch belonged to Buck's close friend, Bull Drenzik, a buddy he met in boot camp. They shipped out from New York on the long voyage to North Africa. Once in combat, Bull shook with nervousness and fear. He told Buck he had a premonition he would die by stepping on a land mine.

Whenever the two were together, everywhere they walked, Buck stepped first and Bull followed in his footsteps. "He felt safe with me," Buck explained.

One day the unit stopped and superiors ordered Buck to fuel up an armored tank. Bull was sent with another group. Engineers pulled out mine detectors, found a German minefield, and marked the area.

When Buck returned to camp, somebody handed him Bull's pocket watch.

In his nervous state, without Buck leading, Bull stepped into the minefield. A mine exploded, tearing his body apart.

Buck carried Bull's pocket watch with him throughout the rest of the war.

He gave everything to the museum, which created a wonderful display.

Several weeks after the museum opened, on a Sunday afternoon, in walked Buck.

"Lee, I have to see the watch," he told me, very agitated. "I have to touch the watch today. I need to touch the watch!"

I walked to the case, opened it and took the watch off the hook. Standing in front of the case, Buck looked at the watch and began stroking it. He began to cry, slowly at first, and then sobbing, his shoulders heaving up and down.

I had never seen a man cry as hard as he did that day and I didn't know what to do. I put my arm around him, and I said, "It's okay, Buck. Let the pain go. Everyone in here understands your pain. Just let it go."

After ten minutes or so, Buck composed himself and put the watch on the hook. He returned many times to look at his display, but he never again asked to touch the watch.

Buck wrote a book sharing his story. It's called *One Soldier's Memories of Death's Head.*

Another time, before the museum officially opened, we were setting up display cabinets when I noticed the same car sitting across the street for a couple of days in a row. The man inside looked at the museum, but never came in.

Then, as I was working on a case, I heard a clunk, clunk, clunk of cowboy boots. Turning to check out the noise, I spied cowboy boots first, worn by a mixed-blood Native American man.

Twentieth century combatants, in front, Jeff Grimes, Persian Gulf; Norman Willard, WWI; Larry Blake, Korean War; and in back, Ron Harmon, Korea/ Vietnam Wars; Buck Winterowd, WWII; Jim Beachboard, Korean War; John Blanchard, Korean War.

"I'm just trying to figure out if this place is for real," he said. "Are you going to do anything for the Indians who have served?"

"I would love to," I told him, "but I have nothing—nothing's been donated to the museum by an American Indian."

"I'm part Indian," he said. "And I have some things. Would you put them in here if I brought them in?"

"Absolutely."

"That's all I wanted to know," he said, then turned and walked away.

A few days later, the same fellow walked in the door, his arms full. He gave us his own Army jacket, his ribbon shirt, Indian artifacts in a frame, and items he'd brought home from the Korean War.

His name was Elwood "Woody" Schabell, a Rochester, Washington, man who served as a medic with the 45th Infantry Division in Korea.

"Let's put these things in this case while you're still here," I told him. I hung the picture frame and uniform as I was talking to him about the Korean War and some of his experiences.

All of a sudden, he quit talking.

I looked around at him. He stood there with his hands out, shaking.

"I can't get the blood off! I can't get the blood off!"

I realized he was having a flashback. I put my arms around him.

"It's okay, Woody," I told him. "It's okay. This is the place to let it go."

He stepped back.

"I've gotta go now," he said. "I can't take it in here anymore. I've gotta go."

Halfway down the aisle, he turned and started walking back to me.

Uh-oh, I thought. *Did I push the wrong button? Is he going to cold-cock me or something?*

"I'll be back," he said, and turning, he walked away.

A few weeks after our emotional encounter, Woody walked in the door. It was close to five o'clock on a Friday. I felt God telling me that Woody wanted to talk. I just locked the door, turned on the "Closed" sign, and stood by the counter. I didn't know what to do, or even what to ask.

"Woody," I said. "Where were you when the firing stopped in Korea?"

"I was up near the front lines," he responded. "We all knew the hour was to come when we were to cease fire, so both sides were throwing everything they could at each other. Then the hour came and the guns fell silent.

"It became so quiet it was almost deafening, if you can understand."

At that point, he stopped, falling to his knees, wailing. I didn't know what to do. *This man's hurting so much!*

I dropped to my knees and put my arms around him.

"It's okay," I said.

He stood up and said, "I gotta go. I gotta get out of here."

"Woody, please don't leave!" I pleaded. "Not in the shape you're in. Please sit down and have a cup of coffee, and we'll talk about something else."

We did. Fifteen minutes later, he left. He was still shaking.

On Sunday afternoon, Woody returned to the museum.

"Woody, how ya doing?" I asked.

"I'm okay," he answered. "But when I got home that night, I was still shaking. My wife told me never, ever to come back to this place.

"But she doesn't understand. My friends are here."

He purchased a bronze memorial plaque honoring four of his best buddies who were killed in Korea. The plaque, placed above the Indian case, reads:

TO THOSE THAT FELL
"Pamamine"
"See You Later"

Pvt. Robert C. Young	Pvt. Ernest R. Roye
Pfc. Richard E. Espinosa	Cpl. Leonard G. Lee

"In here, they're still alive," he continued. "And if my name was on that plaque, I would not want them to forget me, and I will not forget them. So here I am."

He hated the sit-com *MASH*. "I never saw anything funny in a field hospital," he said.

People do not realize it, but God gave me this commission. Sometimes it's hard. Sometimes the emotions just drain you down to nothing, and that's when you need to ask God to lift you back up. There's always something that brings you back to the top again.

Woody has returned many times, carrying the POW flag for us during presentations. Woody told me, "I lost a lot of friends in Korea. Their memories are preserved. This is why Veterans Memorial Museum is so appreciated."

One time a woman and her husband toured the museum. They were both pastors, and halfway through the tour, she asked me, "How can you deal with all this death in here?"

"I don't see it as death," I responded. "I see it as honor, honoring all these men and women who have served. But that's the price of our

Woody Schabell, medic, U.S. Army, 45th Division, in Korea during the Korean War.

freedom. Yes, it is sad. But you just have to deal with it. You can't sweep it under a carpet.

"That's why we're here—to remember. You cannot turn your back on them."

"I don't know how you can do it," she said.

"I know how I can do it—because God gives me the strength when I most need it."

As founder of the museum, I want whoever takes this over to realize that we're not just here showing artifacts. We are here to empathize with those who have served. It takes something special to do that, and it's a hard thing to do.

I wasn't trained to deal with this, but does it take training—or just someone who cares? I don't have special gifts, but I do believe God has given me the gift of love. I don't speak in tongues; I don't see angels; I'm not a prayer warrior or an evangelist. But I do have an open heart.

Sometimes it's a painful gift. But if my heart hurts, what kind of pain are the veterans feeling? I don't suffer one ounce of what they feel. It's hard sometimes to imagine what they carry with them.

Early 1998 Activities

After our grand opening, we helped plan a surprise ninety-ninth birthday for WWI veteran Cpl. Wade LeRoy of Morton. Wade served as a gun commander, Battery E, 65th Coast Artillery at Fort Stevens, Oregon.

When he was only eighteen, Wade LeRoy left to serve in France with his artillery unit as part of the Army Expeditionary Force. During his eighteen months overseas, he was exposed to raw gasoline fumes, which burned his lungs. After the war, he graduated from the University of Washington and worked as a forestry engineer and land surveyor, living in Randle, Washington, for thirty years. He and his wife, Lois, were married for nearly seventy years.

Doug Haughton, who introduced himself as Wade LeRoy's grandson, organized the party. He said they wanted to gather family members and friends in a military setting.

"Were you in the service?" I asked him.

"Yeah, I was in the Army," he responded.

He didn't offer any details. Judging by his age, I figured he served in Vietnam. He didn't want to talk about it, so I didn't press.

WWI veteran Wade LeRoy's ninety-ninth birthday. Son Herb LeRoy is on Wade's left and his brother, Paul LeRoy, is on his right.

Meanwhile, I met one of his uncles, Herb LeRoy, who mentioned that Doug had served in Vietnam and told me to tell him that his old Uncle Herb asked about him.

A few weeks later, Doug, who lived in Allyn, Washington, near Shelton, stopped by the museum to discuss the food, entertainment, and other birthday activities.

"Your Uncle Herb said you're a Vietnam veteran and mentioned that you might have some stuff from Vietnam you might want to share with the museum."

"I've got a bunch of junk left in a box and I'd just as soon leave it there," he said. "It's just a bunch of stuff from Vietnam."

"Well, I understand your thoughts and feelings," I said. "However, wouldn't it be nice to celebrate your grandfather's service in WWI and have a display for your service in Vietnam?"

"No, I don't want to go there," he said.

"I won't ask you again," I said. "The offer is always open."

"No, no, I'm just going to let it go.

Two or three days before the party, who walked around the corner with his arms covered in uniforms, awards, pictures, and medals but Doug? He dropped them on my desk.

"Lee, if you want this junk, you can have it," he said. "It's just the junk I brought home from Vietnam. It's yours. Do what you want with it. Throw it away—I don't care."

"Oh, no, Doug, we'll use it," I said. "That's for sure. We're not going to throw this away."

"Well, you don't have to put it up right away," he said.

We finalized a few more party details and he left. Something inside told me that I needed to assemble his display case right away.

Saturday, March 14, 1998, arrived and so did Wade LeRoy's family.

Since Wade lived in Morton, my wife, Barb, offered to pick him up. She arrived there early and, on the way to Centralia, asked if he knew another WWI veteran who lived in the area, Norman Willard. He didn't, so Barb asked if he'd like to meet him.

"Yes," he responded.

Due to some medical problems, Norman was at Centralia Providence Hospital. Barb took Wade to the dining room, where Norm was, and introduced the two old war veterans. At first they appeared a bit awkward, but then started talking about where each had served. Before long, they were chatting like a couple of old friends. When it was time to leave, Barb noticed Wade sitting beside Norm's chair, and they were holding hands.

Very few WWI veterans were still living at that time. Here were two old boys who once again felt the way they had years ago, when they forged a bond as veterans of a war in a foreign land, a bond that lasts forever, regardless of age.

We must have had a hundred people at Wade's party. Sitting in his wheelchair, Wade clapped his hands, happy and excited.

I looked across the street and saw that Doug Haughton had pulled up in his car, his daughter and wife with him. As they entered the museum, I greeted him and he introduced me to his family.

"Doug, your display is up," I said. "Would you like to see it?"

"Aw, I guess so," he said.

I led the way to a display case with Doug and his wife and daughter following.

He stood in front of it, his fists clenched, one arm encircling his wife, the other around his daughter. As he looked at the case, tears started rolling down his cheeks.

"You don't know what you've done for me today," Doug told me. "In my lifetime, I never believed that my uniform and my medals and my pictures would hang in a place of honor like this."

He told me that when he returned with his unit from Vietnam, they arrived in Washington only to encounter war protesters. They shouted obscenities as the men left Fort Lewis and spit at them as they passed.

"That hurt me so bad," Doug said. Repeating his earlier statement, he said, "You don't know what you have done for me today. I've had my welcome home."

Doug, both a helicopter and fixed-wing pilot, has returned to the museum for many of our Vietnam veterans programs. He's also flown other veterans here. He just loves this place.

We held Wade's one hundredth birthday party at the museum the following year. The Army presented him with an award, and we gave him a Veterans Memorial Museum medal. Four months later, he also received the French Legion of Honor medal, presented by France's representative in Washington, D.C.

By that time, Wade didn't remember a lot about his service overseas, but was proud that he had served his country.

When Wade LeRoy turned 102 on March 14, 2001, we took a large contingent of veterans, in uniform, to the Morton church to help him celebrate. We joined the LeRoys in Morton again in March 2003 to help Wade celebrate his 104th birthday. Wade passed away April 24, 2003.

From left, Marilois LeRoy Haughten (daughter), Rocky LeRoy (son), Herb LeRoy (son), WWI veteran Wade LeRoy, assistant to the French consul, Paul LeRoy (brother), and Jack Cowan, honorary consul of the French government. The consul bestowed the French Legion of Honor medal on Wade LeRoy for his service during World War I.

Chapter Three:

A Full-Time Commitment

IN EARLY 1998, as interest in the museum increased, I found it harder to squeeze time for the museum into my after-work schedule. I was exhausted!

Finally, after much thought, I broached the subject with Barb.

"I either have to just step aside from the museum and let it go, or I have to quit my job, and that cuts our family income in half," I said. "I love them both, but I just physically can't do both."

We faced a huge decision. We weighed the financial security of our family against the desire to build and grow the veterans museum that I felt God had commanded me to do. I felt torn.

"What am I gonna do?" I asked Barb.

"There's no question about it," she responded. "If you feel God has led you to do this, then you quit your job."

"Okay," I said. "If you're agreeable to it, then I'll turn in my resignation tomorrow."

I spoke with my employer, Rick Fisher, who knew about my commitment to the museum and Rick allowed me to use his shop after hours to build the display cabinets.

"I'll work for another month or two," I told Rick. "But I am going to be terminating here shortly and give full commitment to the museum."

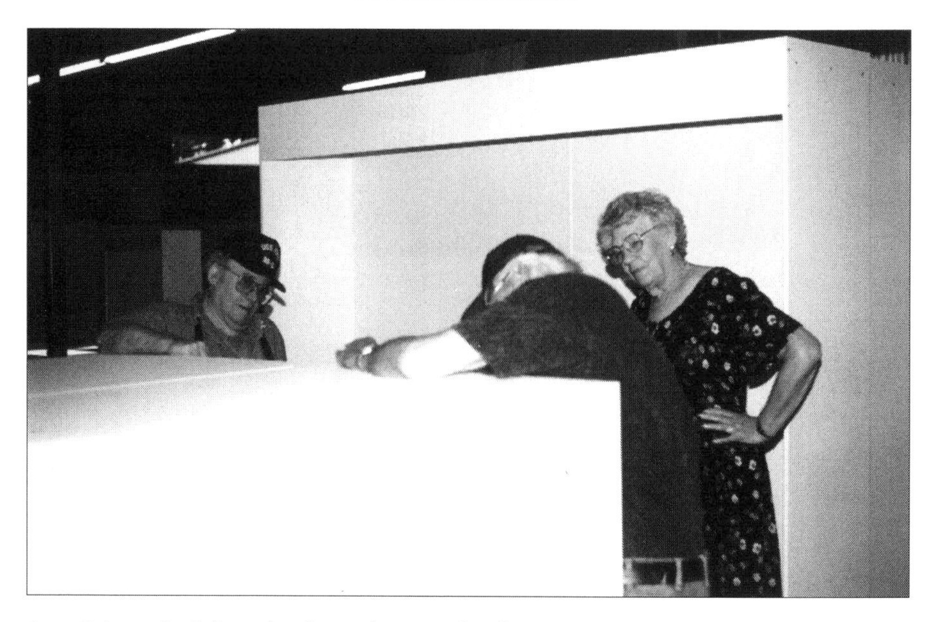

Lee Grimes building display cabinets after hours at Showcase Kitchens in Chehalis, Washington. Supervisors are Larry Blake, left, and Ruby Shepard.

Rick accepted my resignation reluctantly, but he supported our work. As a going-away gift, he created a large wooden road sign that read, "Veterans Memorial Museum, Exit 82," and placed it at the edge of his property adjacent to Interstate 5.

I quit my job in the spring and started working full time at the museum.

At home, during the next six months, we pulled up our bootstraps, tightened our belt buckles to make ends meet, and eliminated any frivolous spending.

About that time, Barb was promoted to a sales job at NC Machinery, which basically doubled her salary. Her income covered the amount that I gave up when I quit my job, almost to the penny. It was incredible.

A lot of people will say that's just coincidence, but we know better. You put your faith in God and he rewards you for your faithfulness, but not always monetarily.

It was another one of those moments when you know that God is with you in this whole project.

I entered the world of museums through a calling from God. I'm not a museumologist or a curator; I'm not trained in the art of museums.

I've read books about properly caring for items, and the board of directors and I have attended seminars. We even hired a consultant to teach us for several hours on how to operate a museum.

After a fifteen-minute tour through the museum, the consultant began his training with these words: "Your museum's going to be a success. I just took a tour with your director; he brought me to tears. Whenever you can bring emotion out in people, they're going to remember it."

I found his professional observations encouraging. We knew we were on the right path, but I wanted to make the museum into an outreach to honor veterans throughout the community, county, state, and beyond.

That's why we started setting aside five special days to honor each group of veterans—POWs and MIAs, Pearl Harbor survivors, WWII, Korean War, and Vietnam War veterans.

The first official event December 7, 1997, commemorated the forty-sixth anniversary of the Japanese attack on Pearl Harbor. Each of the fourteen survivors attending spoke for three or four minutes about what they recalled from that fateful Sunday morning, December 7, 1941. Silence reigned as each survivor shared his thoughts, some with great emotion. Our Pearl Harbor survivors included Walt Engler, Buck Ballou, Howard Gage, C.J. Fox, Vern Jacobson, Cy Simmons, and Dale Gallea.

I remember our first Vietnam Veterans Remembrance Day. Only twenty to thirty Vietnam veterans showed up that first year. We didn't have an official program; we didn't know what to do. The Vietnam vets mingled and visited. We provided a cake and coffee and tours of the museum.

We decided we needed to do more than that, so the second year we held a program. Marine Capt. Roy Simalin, a combat veteran of WWII, Korea, and Vietnam, was the guest speaker. This day was surely to become an annual event.

For two years, we held a Persian Gulf War day to commemorate those who served in that conflict. The first year, ten veterans showed up. The second year, only five came. It was just too soon. We quit holding those days until the time was right.

I remember providing a tour of the museum to retired Master Sergeant Ron Harmon, a Marine who served in Korea and Vietnam and had provided color guard protection for President Dwight D. Eisenhower. He often told about one particular mission, when he was jumpmaster. The plane dropped three nuns by parachute to a Vietnamese school early during the Vietnam War. He held onto the ankles of all three until it was time to jump. A trailing pilot reported seeing their chutes open.

Leading him on a tour, I paused at Harmon's display, which was next to the display case holding Jim Kinsman's Medal of Honor, on permanent loan to the museum.

Whenever Ron Harmon walked past the Medal of Honor, he would salute it.

"Someday I would like to meet this gentleman," he told me.

We always invited Thomas "Jim" Kinsman, the Onalaska man who received the Medal of Honor for throwing himself on a grenade in Vietnam to protect his fellow soldiers. He doesn't attend the events very often.

That first Vietnam Veterans Recognition Day, as the event began, I saw Jim Kinsman across the street. When I approached him, he said he blew a water hose on his car driving into town, and his hands were dirty so he didn't want to attend the event.

"No problem," I told him, encouraging him to enter the building.

I gestured toward Ron.

"Ron, come over here. I want you to meet somebody."

"Who's that?" he asked, closing the space between us.

"Ron Harmon, I'd like to introduce you to Jim Kinsman, Medal of Honor recipient," I said.

Ron snapped to attention and saluted Jim.

"It's an honor to meet you, sir," he said. Then tears seeped from his eyes, flowing down his cheeks. That was the first time I'd ever seen Ron cry. He did an about-face and walked off.

As soon as he left, six or seven other Vietnam vets walked over, stood in a half-circle around Jim, snapped a salute, and said, "It's an honor to meet you, sir." They also began to cry.

Of course, by that time the whole doggone place was crying, except for Jim. I stood behind him, watching everybody else.

After the program ended, I took Jim on a tour of the museum, since he'd never visited before. When we reached his display, I said to him, "Jim, that was quite a reception you got when you came in."

"Yes," he responded. "But I just want to be one of the boys. The medal always seems to come up, and everyone puts me on a pedestal, and I don't want to be there."

We all put him on a pedestal. The man jumped on a hand grenade to save his fellow soldiers!

But the more I thought about it, the more I understood his view. He's an honorable and hardworking man who just wants to be one of the guys who served. It's always interesting to look at things through the eyes of the other person.

At the first Vietnam Veterans Day February 21, 1998, Lee Grimes is seen with Vietnam Medal of Honor recipient Jim Kinsman of Onalaska.

Stan Price and Laurence Mark Rooms in the Museum

We named the museum's library the Laurence Mark Library, after WWII veteran Laurence Mark of Centralia, our first librarian. He possessed an extensive knowledge of military history and donated more than three hundred books to the library. He catalogued by hand all the books we had at the museum, which at that time numbered more than 1,600.

Laurence Mark served in WWII as a machine gunner in the 75th Infantry Division, fighting in the Battle of the Bulge. His brother, Otis Paul Mark, had served in the South Pacific as a Navy Corpsman during the same war. During the Korean War, Paul joined the Army as a medic and was

The Veterans Memorial Museum's first librarian, Laurence Mark, above, and "The Mark Brothers" below, with Paul on left and Laurence on right.

captured by the North Korean Army at the Yalu River near the Chinese border. He was never heard from nor seen again.

Laurence and Paul's uniforms are displayed together on mannequins in the same case, Laurence reaching out to Paul. When Laurence first saw the display, he said, "For the first time in fifty years, I feel like I'm with my brother again." The pain just never goes away. Laurence wrote the following poem in memory of his brother:

Soldier Without a Rifle

In the hard and bitter early days,
You had daring and fearless ways,
That was a special joy of life.
Then the rumors of war were rife.

You left your games of sports and ball,
And was first to answer the clarion call.
Against the enemy when times were trying,
Your skill was to aid the hurt and dying.

Posted to a far foreign land,
To the cold battlefield by high command.
In times of conflict and mortal strife,
The need was aid in preserving life.

You entered without fear or dread,
Across the shell-marked field of the dead.
You trod with your cross of red,
To bring succor to those who had bled.

Without thought of your own comfort and pain,
Your job was to aid those on the frozen plain.
To do your duty as a good soldier must,
To raise the trumpet from the dust.

One more task ... No time to tire,
The wounded had to miss the artillery fire.
The enemy shot from the craggy hill,
Laid your heart forever still ....

Your spirit is now gone forever,
No more will we explore together,
Or ride the plains with one another.
Rest in peace my brother ....

— Copyright ©
Laurence Mark, September 1986

Stan Price was born in Walla Walla, Washington, and worked in the Montesano area before he enlisted in the U.S. Army October 28, 1940. After a short basic training, he was assigned to Battery L., 60th Coast Artillery (AAA) BN, as a heavy machine gunner. His unit departed for the Philippine Islands in November 1940.

Stan's battalion was stationed on Corregidor Island. He volunteered to go to the main island to help train the Philippine Army. Later, Stan was ordered to return to his regular outfit on Corregidor. On their way back to Corregidor, via Bataan, his unit engaged the Japanese in heavy combat and, on April 9, 1942, the U.S. Army surrendered and Stan was taken prisoner by the Japanese army, destined to participate in the horrific Bataan Death March.

The first night of the march, he and two other GIs killed a Japanese guard and escaped to Corregidor in a native canoe they found hidden near the shore. On May 6, 1942, Corregidor fell and, once again, Stan was captured and spent the next forty-two months as a prisoner of war.

Stan spent those three and a half years at Bilibid Prison, Cabanatuan Camp #3, at Nichols Airfield in the Port Area Detail, unloading Japanese supply ships, and at Hanawa, Japan, in an underground copper mine.

Stan recalled the first days in the prison camp after his capture. The guards assigned each prisoner a number in Japanese. The next morning, the guards lined up the prisoners, who were ordered to state their number in Japanese.

As the count moved down the line, one young man did not respond. Stan said he didn't know whether he was being defiant—simply refusing to cave in to his captors' demands—or whether he simply failed to learn his number the previous night.

When the man refused to answer, the Japanese commandant ordered the guards to bring him forward. The commandant had been standing before the prisoners with a three- or four-foot-long two-by-four in his hand, tapping the wood against his leg during the roll call, waiting for something like this to happen.

The guards hauled the American prisoner forward and the commandant then took that two-by-four and beat him to death. Stan told me what hurt him the most was that it took so long for that young man to die.

Then, the roll call continued.

Another morning when the American prisoners lined up to recite their numbers, one man failed to sound off. He wasn't in the formation, so the commandant stopped the count and instructed the guards to check his hut to see if he was sick or unable to come for some reason. They didn't find him in the hut. They checked the hospital. They even checked the slit trenches where the men did their daily constitutionals. They couldn't find him in the camp and, in fact, the man had escaped the previous night.

Upon hearing the results of the search, the commandant ordered the prisoners to sound off again and told every tenth man to step forward. Stan knew at that point some sort of retaliation would take place. As the count moved down the line, Stan watched every tenth man step forward. He remembered thinking, "Am I going to be one of the ten?" As luck would have it, he said, the man three down from him stepped forward. "I felt so relieved," he said, "but I felt so sorry for those ten men."

When the commandant saw ten men standing there, he ordered the guards to bring them forward. He turned them around, forced them onto their hands and knees, and ordered the guards to draw their swords—and cut their heads off on the spot, which they did.

He then stood on his stool and told the prisoners in his very broken English, "One man escape, ten men die!" It was called the rule of ten, a technique to keep the prisoners in line, and Stan said it worked very well because nobody ever escaped from the camp again. As a reminder for the prisoners, the commandant had the heads of those ten men erected on tall stakes around the camp to keep in their minds the penalty of escape.

While at Nichols Airfield, Stan and the prisoners worked on the airfield picking up rocks, putting them into old coal cars, and pushing the cars full of rocks to a dumping site. The cars had no rails to travel on; they had to be pushed by hand through the dirt and mud. One guard thought the handful of guys pushing the car failed to work hard enough. He struck Stan across his back with a pickax handle hard enough to rupture his kidney. His injury swelled him like a balloon; he thought his kidney would burst. He couldn't even walk and, since he couldn't work, he received only half rations. Prisoners who worked received a half cup of rice a day. If they were sick and couldn't work, they'd receive half as much.

To survive, he pulled himself across the compound on his elbows to a nail shack where prisoners worked pounding raw iron ingots. His captors gave him a hammer and anvil and he hammered them into spikes so he'd receive full rice rations.

Miraculously his kidney healed.

As the war wore on, many prisoners were sent to the Japanese mainland to work in mines as slave laborers.

Stan was ordered aboard a Japanese ship—what was known as a Hell Ship because of the cramped and squalid conditions, lack of food, air and water, and cruelty of the crew. Allied bombers and submarines targeted these ships, firing at them without realizing American prisoners were aboard. Many American POWs died as a result of these attacks.

When Stan boarded, he climbed down a ladder into the hold of the ship. Approximately 1,500 men were crammed into one compartment. They lined up in rows, the front of one man to the back of another. They sat down and the man behind would spread his legs so the man in front could lean against his chest. The man in the back of the row would lean against the ship's bulkhead. This is how they would sleep, if possible. There was about a four-foot space at the foot of the ladder where a bucket was lowered on a rope. The bucket was to be used as a latrine. Their daily ration of one cup of water and two tablespoons of rice per day was handled in the same manner. The problem with this was the prisoners near the bucket could use it, but then men in the outer sections couldn't reach the bucket in time. Men had to sit in their own filth, the air rancid and stifling, the heat unbearable. Many men died each night; they were buried at sea the next morning, without ceremony.

The hatch opening had a steel mesh padlock on it so nobody could get out. The ship had sugar, flour, gas, and machinery aboard for the Japanese military. One day a fire broke out in the equipment hold. The men didn't know if it was close to the gasoline or not, but they knew they were locked in with no way of getting out. The fire was extinguished but it was a frantic and frightening time for the POWs.

When he reached northern Japan, the enemy forced Stan to work in an underground copper mine near Hanawa. He was mechanically adept, so the Japanese made him work on the equipment. One time, as he was working on a large bearing in an ore crusher, the huge bearing cap slipped as they were trying to reset it, crushing his thumbs. He was allowed to see a Japanese military doctor, who laughed at him. The doctor took pliers and yanked off the remnants of his thumb nails. They grew back.

The men shivered with cold at night in their prison huts. Their captors added makeshift stoves, but the men had nothing to burn.

Early each morning, their captors marched the prisoners on their eleven-mile journey over the snow to the underground mine, where they'd strip down to a G-string and straw sandals to survive the sweltering heat from the smelter. There was a large pile of coal near the smelter.

Stan kept eyeing the coal pile. He had found a small sack, which he tucked inside his G-string. When the guards looked away, he stuffed coal into the sack. He got away with it and they burned the coal that night; it didn't put out a lot of heat but the flames seemed to warm them psychologically.

Stan thought that was pretty easy so the next day he looked around until the opportune time presented itself, stooped down, and tucked coal into the sack. Then he felt a tap on his shoulder. A Japanese guard stood over him.

In broken English, the guard demanded, "You apologize for stealing from imperial Japanese army."

Emaciated, frustrated and angry, Stan reacted. He stood up and looking the guard square in the eye, he said, "You slant-eyed son-of-a-bitch! I will apologize to you for nothing."

It was the wrong thing to say but Stan said it made him feel better to let his feelings out.

The guard grabbed a scoop shovel from the coal pile and struck Stan across the back, knocking him down. Stan pulled himself back to his feet, looked the guard square in the eye, and didn't say a word.

"He took that scoop shovel and hit me again, knocked me back down," Stan told me. "I got back up, looked him square in the eye, didn't say a word. He hit me again, knocked me back down."

After six or eight blows, the guard broke him.

"Physically, I could not get back up on my own."

Two guards lifted him by the arms and dragged him outside to the mine's entrance. Snow covered the ground. They dragged him to a guard shack, still wearing a G-string and straw sandals, and ordered him to stand without moving.

"I stood there all night long," Stan told me during our interview, "but I moved, jumped up and down, beat on myself to keep my circulation going. It was the longest night of my life and I was not going to give up.

"I might die, but I'm not going to let them kill me."

Stan saw many guys die when they lost the will to live. They just couldn't take it anymore.

When dawn broke the next day, much to their surprise, the guards found him still alive so they returned him to the mine to work.

One Japanese mine foreman felt sympathy for the prisoners. He'd smuggle them apples, gum, cigarettes, and candy. Each time his superiors caught him, they beat him as badly as they did the American prisoners. When the war ended, Stan was working in the mine. A Japanese foreman told Stan and a couple of other prisoners to follow him. He took them out of the mine and, instead of heading back to the camp, took them on a long walk that ended at a farmhouse. The Japanese foreman told them this was his home; he fed the men and gave them a bed to sleep in. The next day he took the prisoners to Hanawa and turned them over to an American officer. The war had been over for many days and the foreman wanted to do something kind for these men. Stan said he and the Japanese man exchanged cards around Christmastime once a year until the Japanese man died.

Stan's freedom came on September 17, 1945. At the time of his release, he weighed 109 pounds; his normal weight was 180 pounds. Stan also served in the Army during the Korean War. I asked Stan, "What would have happened if you had been taken prisoner again in Korea?" He responded, "That would never have happened."

When I first met Stan, I saw a kindly man whose mannerisms belied his experience. To look at him, you'd never know he had witnessed beheadings and endured what he had. I told him about my vision of opening the museum and my desire to record veterans' stories.

"No, sir, I can't do that," he responded when I asked for an interview. "I won't grant you an interview. I've tried to forget this all my life."

"Stan," I said, "I understand and I will not ask you again. The offer is always open. I do want to leave you with one thought. As a veteran of the military, you all have a story to tell. Each story is as important as the others. Your story is unique to American history.

"Does your family know what you went through?"

Stan and his wife had two daughters; they knew only bits and pieces of his story. His wife knew more, but I don't think anybody really knew the whole story.

Stan Price with his wife, Joyce, in front of his display at the First Church of God's Patriotic Program.

I said to him, "As a POW, it had to affect and change your life. Your family needs to know what you went through to understand you better. Here's my phone number. If you wish to, give me call."

Three weeks later, the phone rang. It was Stan.

"Would you mind coming over?" he asked. "I think I'd like to talk to you."

I made a beeline for his house!

"I'm going to tell you my story," he said. "What I'm about to tell you, I want no pity or sympathy for. It was my lot in life, being there serving my country, and I have accepted that. But I never want America—especially young people—to forget one thing: the price of freedom. On that basis I will tell you my story."

As his story unfolded, I could hardly believe what I was hearing. Afterward, I made a copy of the interview for his family. His wife, Joyce, thanked me.

"He still has severe nightmares from his POW days," she told me. "But it seems like after he told you his story his nightmares have diminished. They've not gone away, but they're not as severe as they were."

Stan Price died August 3, 1997.

We hold a special day at the museum to honor those who served as Prisoners of War and those who were listed as Missing in Action.

HELPING A TROUBLED YOUNG WOMAN

At our grand opening I had met a young female Army veteran, Carrie Danner-Dixon, who was a truck driver in Somalia. She had figured she was on a peacekeeping mission, bringing supplies, medicine, food, and clothing to the people of Somalia.

But when her convoy was attacked, she fired back and some Somalis died. That tormented her. So did the vision seen on television of the captured American who was dismembered and paraded around Mogadishu. She was a casualty of that conflict.

Barb and I tried to help this troubled kindhearted young woman in any way we could. But we felt so helpless.

One day a Scandinavian man who lived in Onalaska, Washington, stopped by the museum for the first time. I greeted him.

"God told me to come here today, and I don't know why," he said. "Here I am."

I asked him a couple of questions. "Are you a veteran?"

Carrie Danner-Dixon, a Somalia veteran and first webmaster of the Veterans Memorial Museum.

"Yes."

"What do you do?"

"I'm a psychologist. Do you have a veteran who is in real need of a counselor?"

"Yes," I said. "We do. There is a young lady here who served in combat in Somalia who is in real need of someone to talk to."

"Then that's why I'm here today," he said. "Will you introduce me to her?"

I connected the two of them and they began meeting.

Faith and Healing

Another time, a vanload of primarily Vietnam veterans suffering from Post-Traumatic Stress Disorder visited the museum from American Lake Veterans Hospital in Tacoma, Washington. They wanted to look through the museum on their own, rather than with a tour guide.

I saw a Native American man standing alone in an aisle. I walked down to speak to him.

"Are you a Christian?" he asked.

"Yes, I am," I responded.

"I thought so," he said. "I felt the presence in here when I walked in. I am, too."

I told him about how the museum started and why I felt called by God to devote my life to it. "There's something very special in here that I can feel," he said.

We don't evangelize at the museum. We lead by example. Sometimes it's subtle; other times people need someone to listen who cares. But usually our faith is shared just by leading a good life yourself.

The Lord knows I've got a lot of bumps in my road. It's bumpy and I've failed a lot in my life. But I cannot fail in this one.

In 1998 I was asked to be the guest speaker at the U.S. Army 50th General Hospital Association's reunion, which took place in the Officers' Club at Fort Lewis, Washington. The opportunity to speak to such an elite group was exciting yet a bit challenging too. How could I relate to these medical men and women, a majority of them retired officers? They requested that I speak about the Veterans Memorial Museum, what we were about, future plans, and so on. I prepared my twenty- to thirty-minute speech and Barb and I drove to Fort Lewis. We were checked in at the gate and found our destination. Fort Lewis is a huge base and the grounds are beautifully kept.

A wonderful dinner was served and then it came time for my presentation. I was extremely nervous as it started, hoping and praying that my presentation would be well received. I wondered how I could relate to these people who had set up a hospital in Saudi Arabia during Operation Desert Storm. The lineage of the 50th General goes back to WWI and WWII as a 1,000-bed field hospital in France in both wars. I decided to speak on how the museum had already healed or, at the minimum, relieved some of the pain from hurting veterans. I shared several individual stories, many related here in this book. Several times I felt myself choking up, especially when I saw a tear falling from the cheeks of the 50th veterans in the audience. I finished my presentation with my poem, "Who Will Remember?" At the conclusion of my presentation, I received a standing ovation and there was hardly a dry eye in the crowd.

Col. Tom Hutchinson, who was the commander of the 50th General in Saudi Arabia and president of the reunion group, walked up to the podium. I will never forget his words, "Lee, we have decided that you and your wife Barb are one of us. We have healed the bodies where you have healed the hearts. We want to make you and Barb honorary lifetime members of the 50th General Hospital."

Wow, then the tears flowed down Barb's and my cheeks. To be accepted into this circle of veterans was almost too good to believe. It was one of the highlights of my life and I am sure Barb's too. A couple of years later we invited Dale Ingle and his wife, Linda, to accompany us to the annual 50th General Hospital Association's reunion and they readily accepted. We all now make this an annual event, greeting our newfound friends once again. In 2002 they bestowed upon me the honor of Volunteer of the Year from within their ranks, another honor that ranks very high on my personal list.

Chapter Four:

Who Is This Guy?

NOBODY WOULD HAVE FIGURED THE LONELY BOY who played baseball by himself on a farm and cattle ranch in South Dakota would someday launch a highly acclaimed regional museum to honor and heal American veterans.

But God does work miracles.

My parents were already grandparents when I was born in 1948. My sister, Melva, was twenty-two, Allen was eleven, and Gene was eight. I had a niece and nephew older than me.

Life on a ranch consisted of work and more work. Once in a while we'd visit neighboring farm families so the adults could play cards. The families worked together in threshing bees, shocking oats during harvest, and branding calves. The threshing bee was the year's great social event.

But for me it was a lonely life. Our closest neighbor with kids lived ten miles away. On those rare occasions when I wasn't working, I'd play baseball: I'd hit the ball and race after it myself, bring it back to my makeshift home plate, and do it all over again.

My father instilled a work ethic and a lasting principle in me: You never ask for anything from anyone; you earn it. That proved a hindrance when we started the museum, because in the back of my mind, I was not doing anything to earn the money when I asked people to donate.

My mother was a schoolteacher. When I started first grade in 1954, Mom was my teacher for the first two years. Needless to say, I was the teacher's pet! The school was in Scranton, North Dakota, which was twenty-five miles from the family farm. During the week Mom and I would stay in town in a small house that had belonged to her parents. On the weekends and during the summer we would go to the farm. In 1959 Mom took a teaching position at the Lanesboro School in South Dakota, a one-room country schoolhouse that was about seven or eight miles from the farm. I attended that school for my sixth grade. A short time later, my brother Allen and his wife, Patsy, bought the family farm and Mom, Dad, and I all lived in town.

I worked during my high school years at a four-lane bowling alley called Lucky 4 Lanes. Before going to school, I would wash and buff the floor, pick up pop and beer bottles, and do whatever was needed to keep that place looking shipshape. I began bowling at age fifteen and have never lost my love for the game.

After I graduated from Scranton High School in 1966, I signed up for selective service but was classified as 4-F because of a heart murmur and ulcers. I developed the ulcers as a teenager because I kept my feelings inside, where they gnawed at me, and eventually ate my stomach up. The heart murmur was the result of rheumatic fever I contracted as a child. I still have the heart murmur.

In 1966, I enrolled as a freshman at the University of North Dakota in Grand Forks. It was a beautiful campus but the winters were bitter cold. Sitting in the Red River Valley next to the North Dakota-Minnesota border, the wind would come howling down from Canada. It snowed a lot and the temperatures would often be twenty degrees below zero or colder. With the wind-chill factor, you didn't stay outside very long. I lived in a men's dormitory, McVey Hall, a few blocks from the main campus. In the bad winters they constructed mobile tunnels out of corrugated steel to walk through. The days at the university were one of life's memorable times with lots of hard studying, great sports teams to watch, and plenty of fun on weekends. Oh, to be young again!

One of my highlights in college was taking flying lessons. I flew a Cessna 150, which was tricky with all the winds that blow in Dakota. You learned quickly how to slip your way into a landing. I remember during my first solo flight, my heart was pounding as I took off. Now it was all up to me; I had no instructor to bail me out. But the flight went well and I enjoyed many other solo flights afterward. I had passed the Federal Aviation Administration's written exam and needed only ten more flight hours to obtain my pilot's license. The lessons were expensive and, since I was paying my own way through school, I ran out of money so stopped my lessons short. Although I had two years to acquire the additional ten hours, I never flew again.

I never drank much in college, where I saw what drinking could do to people. I grew sick every time I drank. My father had been an alcoholic who quit drinking when I was about ten.

My parents loaned me a thousand dollars for college and I applied for other loans too. I repaid every penny of the $6,700 it cost me, working construction and railroad jobs during the summer and food services positions at the university during the school year. I even ironed clothes for other students for twenty-five cents per garment. There are always ways to make extra money when you really think about it.

I graduated in 1970 with a bachelor of science degree in business administration with a minor in accounting. I also had taken every computer programming course offered at that early time of computers. Much to my surprise I received an invitation to interview for one of two highly competitive computer programming jobs with Sears and Roebuck.

They flew me to Chicago where my interview was conducted at the company headquarters. In the morning I took a cab from the Hilton Hotel to the Sears Tower. At that time, Chicago was a hotbed for civil rights and many young people protested U.S. involvement in Vietnam. As the black cab driver navigated through the turbulent city streets, I watched as people raised their fists in the air; the driver responded, shoving his fist out the window in agreement. It was an eye-opener for this country boy!

The job was to be in a windowless room with a mainframe computer and each programmer had a very small cubicle for his office. Being used to the wide-open prairies, this seemed very claustrophobic. I felt honored a few weeks later to receive a letter saying I had been accepted for one of the positions. However, I didn't like the big city with all its unrest so I returned to my hometown of Scranton, North Dakota, and accepted a job as a management trainee for Farmland Industries.

A few months later, my brother, Gene, who worked in Glasgow, Montana, told me the Air Force base was being vacated and a private company, Avco Corp., working under a government contract, was hiring people to maintain the base in a state of readiness. The Army section of the Air Force base needed a cost accountant.

I remember the day in February 1971 when I walked into the brick administration building to interview for the job. Looking down a long corridor lined with offices, I saw a light shining through a door at the end of the hallway, clearly outlining the silhouette of a woman with long, beautiful legs. I remember thinking, *The man who gets her is one lucky guy.*

I married her nine months later.

As a young man, I fell in love with every girl I saw. I even became engaged once, but my fiancée got cold feet, leaving me brokenhearted.

But then I met that long-legged woman—Barb Prestegord, a bookkeeper from Twin Valley, Minnesota, and a divorced mother with a young son, Jeffrey.

On my twenty-third birthday in April, Barb brought me a cupcake with a candle. We started dating in September and married November 13, 1971.

Shortly after our wedding, Avco lost its government contract. The company offered me a job in Saudi Arabia. Barb and I discussed the offer. Discussing our futures, I told her, "I always wanted to be a professional bowler." I thought I had potential.

She said, "Whatever you want to do, I'll support you."

We turned down the Saudi offer, quit our jobs, and moved to Aurora, Colorado, where I took a position with Brunswick Corp. as an assistant manager in a huge bowling alley. I didn't like the hours and never had time to bowl. And, as a small-town boy, I didn't like the big city.

Six months later, we moved back to North Dakota, where I started working in the fall of 1972 as chief clerk and bookkeeper for the Knife River Coal Mining Co., a surface coal mine that produced a hundred cars of lignite coal per day for a coal-fired plant in South Dakota.

VISITING THE PACIFIC NORTHWEST

In 1977, we visited Barb's sister, Arlene, who lived on Middle Fork Road in Chehalis, Washington, with her husband, Don Roberts, nephew of Loren and Patti Estep.

I never saw so much green as I did when we visited the Pacific Northwest; it was gorgeous.

Loren Estep took me salmon fishing on an ocean charter. Although I had seen the ocean during a 1959 visit to California and the Northwest, I had never been on a boat on the ocean.

"Don't feel bad if you get seasick," Loren warned me. A WWII Navy veteran, Loren told me the waves never bother him.

The first one to get seasick that day was Loren!

After returning to North Dakota, I kept thinking how nice it was in Washington. But Barb's parents lived in Minnesota, so I figured she wouldn't want to move.

Finally, in November 1977, I mentioned to Barb that I had thought of moving to Washington, and she said she had been thinking the same thing, but figured I wouldn't want to move away from my folks in Scranton.

In December 1977, we visited Arlene again, this time looking for jobs. I told Barb, "If we both find jobs and a place to live, I know it will be God's will." Arlene's husband, Don Roberts, knew Wayne Anderson, who hired me as a carpenter for his housing construction company. Barb obtained a service clerk job at NC Machinery, a dealer for Caterpillar that also sold parts and repaired equipment. They also sold new and used equipment at multiple locations.

We bought a trailer house near Don and Arlene's on Middle Fork Road, then returned to North Dakota to sell our house. It took only a month to sell it in a small town where nothing ever sold.

My father asked, "What in the hell do you want to move out to that godforsaken country for?"

Two years later, he visited and wanted to move here. But he passed away before he had the chance.

Moving to Chehalis

In early February 1978, we packed to leave, but a storm-of-the-century blizzard delayed us several days, burying our house in drifts. It took a couple of days to clear the roads and dig ourselves out so we could drive a U-Haul to our front door. Barb called the state patrol and they confirmed that Highway 12 was open to Montana.

We loaded the U-Haul and left, but twenty miles from home, traffic halted as truckers shoveled snow to clear a mile-and-a-half-long drift. At the top of the hill, a farmer with a front-end loader moved snow, heading our direction. We shoveled with them until the road was clear, three and a half hours later, and then drove to the Montana border forty miles away. We followed rotary snowplows as they cleared the road. At one point, Barb blinked her lights because she couldn't steer; snow had packed so hard in the fender wells of our '76 Monte Carlo that the tires couldn't move sideways. After chipping the snowpacks loose with a tire iron, we moved on.

Snowbanks on Highway 12 at North Dakota-Montana border in February 1978. Barb took the picture from inside the car.

It took four days to reach Washington, and we arrived at Snoqualmie Pass Sunday night at the height of ski season, driving forty miles an hour up and down the hills while traffic backed up behind us. I pulled off to let faster cars pass, then took the Auburn cutoff south. With cars still behind me, I saw a hill that looked like it rose forever. I prayed, asking God for help, and that U-Haul raced uphill sixty miles an hour. Barb couldn't understand why I was driving so fast. I said, "God's hand just gave me a little push!"

We started working shortly after we arrived. After three or four months, I landed a job with Ken's Kustom Kabinets in Chehalis. I worked for him eight years and then he sold the business to Rick Fisher, who changed the name to Showcase Kitchens. I worked for Rick about twelve years. Altogether, I worked as a cabinetmaker for twenty years.

Barb worked at NC Machinery twenty-four years, serving as branch administrator and telemarketing rep before entering sales in a male-dominated field. But the more people said she would fail, the more determined she became to make it. She was very successful.

I've always had the Lord on my heart. Growing up on the prairie, seeing nature and beauty, I always knew there was a God. I learned catechism at the Lutheran Church in Scranton.

I used to question my decisions in life. So often when we face what seem like disappointments in life, we truly are gently being led.

I always loved Billy Graham. As a young man one night, I watched the televangelist at a revival, where he invited people to give their hearts to the Lord. I dropped to my knees in front of the television and asked Jesus to come into my heart.

Barb knew God before I met her, which helped her survive a tough childhood with an alcoholic father. Barb's mother, Betty, held the family together and, as a result, Barb's sister, brother, and mother are extremely close today.

I had told myself if I ever got the opportunity to renew my vows personally, I would. Shortly after we moved to Washington, Billy Graham held a crusade at the Tacoma Dome.

We attended and he gave an invitation to come forward.

With Barb on my right arm and Jeff, who was twelve or thirteen, on my left, we walked down the aisle, filled with the Holy Spirit. The hair on the back of my neck lifted, goose bumps prickled my body, and I felt chilled but not cold. My whole body just felt full of joy. I was ecstatic.

One time, while sitting in my car, I felt the Lord beside me. I even touched the seat because I felt so sure that he was there. I felt excited and uplifted and then he was gone.

Another day, while replacing the front tie rods under an old 1964 Comet Caliente, I struggled to break loose the old bolts. Angry and frustrated, I let loose a few choice words, but then realized Jeff was beside me. I asked him to crawl beneath the car and we put our hands on the tie rod and asked God to help remove it. We took our hands off, I hit it once, and it just fell. Jeff was there to witness the power of prayer.

That's how I recognized the presence of the Lord during the wee hours of the morning that joyous day when I received the call to preserve the stories of veterans.

A lot of things have given me strength to achieve in life, especially the knowledge, or insight, to know when God has given me a command.

Chapter Five:

Visitors from Afar

As we settled into the museum, we saw phenomenal growth as word spread about the place that honors veterans for their service.

David Whitney, a Florida man had helped organize reunions for the Army Security Agency, told us that he possessed a 7.7 mm Japanese Arisaka Type 99 rifle, a common weapon used during WWII. He asked if he could give the weapon as a "peace donation" in honor of Tohru Shimizu, a wonderful Japanese man he had met many years earlier through Rotary International.

Tohru Shimizu served in the Japanese military during WWII, in the equivalent of our West Point, but the war ended before he entered active military service.

Afterward, as his lifelong ambition, Shimizu traveled many places, promoting world peace wherever he went.

We agreed to accept the rifle in honor of Shimizu and his peace-keeping efforts. Mr. Whitney mailed us the weapon through an authorized weapons dealer. David Whitney sent along two small brass plaques explaining that the rifle is a peace donation in Shimizu's honor. They read as follows:

"A Peace Donation"

This World War II Japanese 7.7 Arisaka Type 99 rifle has been donated
to the Veterans Memorial Museum in honor of
Mr. Tohru Shimizu
Kanagawa, Japan
Who has spent over 50 years promoting peace between
the United States and Japan.
Donated by Mr. David Whitney, Marathon Shores, FL

I sent a letter to Mr. Shimizu, along with one of the brass plaques, explaining the gift we had received in his honor.

On January 29, 2000, I received a phone call from a man who spoke in broken English.

"My name Tohru Shimizu, in Seattle for Rotary convention," he said. "Like to come to museum to see rifle in my honor."

We were surprised and excited that he was in Washington state. I offered to pick him up and drive him south to Chehalis.

"No, I will take train," he said. He planned to arrive the following day.

Immediately, I contacted the three Rotary presidents in our local area and our museum's board of directors, inviting them to meet Mr. Shimizu. This was our first international visitor!

One of our board members, Cy Simmons, had served aboard the USS *Oklahoma* when it was docked at Pearl Harbor December 7, 1941. The Japanese bombed the *Oklahoma*, and 237 sailors on his ship perished, in addition to all the other Americans killed in the attack on Pearl Harbor.

When I invited Cy to the museum, he replied rather gruffly. "Why would I want to meet that slant-eyed SOB?"

"That's okay," I told him. "You don't need to be there. However, we are going to honor this man when he is here."

I invited Vern Jacobson of Winlock, who served on the USS *California* at Pearl Harbor. He had married a Japanese woman, Emiko, during the occupation of Japan in the early 1950s.

"Yes, I would like to come and meet this man," he said.

We knew what time he'd arrive at the Centralia train station. Barb and I waited for him and watched a short Japanese gentleman wearing glasses step off the train.

We introduced ourselves, and he was very polite, bowing to us in typical Japanese tradition. We drove to the museum.

The first two people to greet this man at the door were Vern Jacobson and Cy Simmons. In the back of my mind, I wondered, *How is this going to go?*

I introduced the two men to Mr. Shimizu as Pearl Harbor survivors.

He immediately bowed at the waist and said, "Soooo sorry."

He wouldn't stand up, but remained bowed. Vern said, "Sir, there's no need for that. The war is over."

That just seemed to cut the ice. We introduced our guest to the rest of the people at the museum. We drank coffee and ate refreshments and then I took him on a tour through the museum. We had a lot of Japanese war memorabilia displayed, so I asked if he could interpret any of the writings on the flags, scarves, and other items.

He explained about the items, written in a different dialect than he spoke, which listed the names of the owner's friends and family. He said people who worked in factories would sign silk scarves or flags as good luck items from home for soldiers to carry into combat.

"How do you feel about seeing Japanese artifacts in an American military museum?" I asked.

"They are simply spoils of war, nothing more," he said.

"But the one thing I see in your museum is great honor: You have honored your people who have served your country, and I see the honor in here."

As we continued touring the museum, we stopped at a case displaying items loaned by the wife of a Winlock soldier who had passed away. Her husband had obtained the items in the South Pacific during WWII.

One of the items was a cloth waist belt of a thousand knots, made by Japanese families for their soldiers. Ten family members and friends sewed a hundred knots each onto the belt, creating a thousand knots, which was considered a good luck number in the Japanese culture.

The Winlock soldier shot a Japanese sniper out of a tree and took his personal items, including the waist belt, as souvenirs of war. He also took the man's wallet, which had American military insignia attached to it and contained Japanese money. It was done on both sides, right or wrong. That's what happens in war.

Also inside the wallet he found a business card ... and a family photo.

The American soldier's wife indicated that it would be nice someday if the picture could be returned to the Japanese family.

So I asked Shimizu if the business card and photograph could be tracked. He said the business card represented a factory that operated in the 1940s. I gave him a copy of the items and kept the originals.

We visited a bit longer and he mingled with the other veterans. Cy came up to me.

"Lee, would you take my picture with Mr. Shimizu shaking my hand back there by his rifle?"

I was happy to do so. This was another healing in a sense. These men represented two enemies at one time. It was a wonderful humanitarian thing to see.

Before he left the museum, Mr. Shimizu pulled out four crisp one-hundred-dollar bills.

"This is for your museum," he said.

That was quite a gesture on behalf of a military veteran from Japan.

Left to right, Pearl Harbor survivors Cy Simmons, USS Oklahoma, *and Vern Jacobson, USS* California, *with Tohru Shimizu and WWII Navy veteran Loren Estep, who served on the USS* Steamer Bay.

We left the museum and treated Mr. Shimizu to dinner at Mary McCrank's before returning him to the train station. We learned more about his family and history, including the successful grocery and house-cleaning businesses he and his wife ran and his quest to promote peace.

After returning to Japan, Mr. Shimizu emailed me to ask if he could become a life member of the museum. It cost $750, with the money set aside to raise money for a new building. Mr. Shimizu wired us $1,000. He's still our only international lifetime member.

A few weeks later, I received another email from Tohru Shimizu.

"I have located his daughter," he wrote, referring to the photo of the Japanese family. He worked through the company records to find the man's dependents.

We spoke with the Winlock soldier's wife, who wanted us to return at least the photo and the card. We made copies and carefully boxed the two originals and mailed them to Shimizu, who had worked through the Chamber of Commerce in the community where the daughter lived to arrange a presentation returning her father's items.

She wrote a short letter to us.

"Thank you for the return of the items," she said. "Hopefully this heals the scars of many years ago."

She signed it.

She probably never knew the details of how her father had died in the war. So many Japanese soldiers died in the jungle, many buried in mass graves. Sixty years after the war, at least a personal part of her father had been returned to her.

It turned out that she was not in the photograph. Neither was her mother. Sometimes maybe it's better to let things lie. However, the business card was from the factory where he had worked. The card was placed on the family shrine in her home.

We still correspond with Mr. Shimizu. We send him the newsletter and email each other. It's just been an honor to get to know him.

Visitors to the Museum

One day a sweet little lady of about eighty entered the museum. I introduced myself.

She responded that she was Marguerite Jasper from New York and had served as a Navy nurse during WWII. She was neatly dressed and looked like anybody's grandmother, her grey hair put up into a bun. Her smile would melt the coldest heart. I took her on a tour and she was tremendously interested. As we progressed, I began asking her a few questions. Her responses were very moving and, at the end of the tour, I asked her if she would sit for a video interview and share her story.

"I've never done anything like that, but I'm pleased that you think my story is interesting enough to listen to," she said. She was on her way to Seattle to visit family but would be back in a few days.

A few days later, she returned to the museum to share her story.

Marguerite Jasper, a WWII U.S. Navy nurse, in October 2001.

Trained as a nurse in the States, she shipped overseas to the South Pacific island of Espiritu Santos. She was among the first nurses to arrive and many of the Navy guys swarmed the dock to see the young nurses.

As time passed, LST-267 came into port for repairs and Marguerite and the seven nurses in her hut received an invitation to dinner from the captain. They accepted the invitation and donned summer dress uniforms, which were skirts. Aboard the LST, they started climbing upstairs to the galley, while guys stood below ogling them and peeking beneath their skirts.

"Lieutenant," one of the nurses said, "All these guys are looking up our skirts as we're going up the ladders."

"Don't worry about it. It's been so long since these guys have seen a nice pair of legs," the lieutenant responded. "It's not going to hurt to let them take a peek or two."

Marguerite met a young man, Lt. Jasper, aboard the LST and a mutual admiration grew. They were married at the end of the war.

Working in a hospital, Marguerite remembered when a United Service Organization, or USO, troupe arrived, including Bob Hope and comedian Jerry Colonna. One of the boys in the hospital had wraps covering his eyes. Jerry Colonna asked Marguerite what happened and she explained that the young man was only sixteen years old and had lost his sight and a leg. The entertainer and Marguerite drifted out to the hospital balcony where Jerry Colonna sobbed. The sight of these wounded young men overwhelmed him.

She was so grateful for the entertainers who lifted the spirits of the wounded servicemen.

As she told a story, Marguerite would cry. She'd tell another story and laugh. She never let herself get down. The entire interview was like a roller coaster ride, up and down, one minute crying, the next laughing. She died a few years ago and we really miss her.

Another encounter at the museum I will never forget.

Sylvia Winterowd, a Rochester woman who was undergoing chemotherapy for leukemia, visited the museum to see her husband's display. She had lost her hair and wasn't very strong physically, but she wanted a tour.

I led her through the museum, explaining what we saw in each case.

Then we reached the display case showing the Glenn Miller Orchestra and our own local member of the band, Erwin "Whitey" Thomas, who lived in Mossyrock, Washington, before moving to California.

Whitey, who received the nickname as a child because of his blond hair, learned to play the trumpet at the age of six, and performed on the trumpet with his town's band by the time he was ten.

As a teenager, he filled in briefly with the Glenn Miller Orchestra to help out a friend, and later he performed professionally before joining the Army. When he was stationed at Fort Bragg, he received a call from Miller. The famous band director told Whitey he needed a good trumpet player, so the twenty-two-year-old joined Miller's Army Air Force Band. The purpose was to provide entertainment for servicemen overseas.

Whitey performed with the band from 1943 to 1945, and he was the last band member to speak to Miller before the director disappeared over the English Channel on a cold and foggy morning December 15, 1944.

Whitey, who also performed with Count Bassie, The Dorsey Brothers, and Benny Goodman, donated to the museum many of his

Whitey Thomas playing "swing tunes" at the WWII dinner and dance on his valve trombone.

mementos from his days with Glenn Miller. In addition to photographs, medals, and original programs, the display features a copy of a letter that Glenn Miller wrote to his brother eleven days before he disappeared, saying prophetically, "By the time you receive this, we should be in Paris—barring, of course, a nosedive into the channel."

During her visit, as Sylvia gazed at the display case, she exclaimed, "Oh, I remember the Glenn Miller band. I always wished I could dance with one of the members of the band. I'm sure they must have been fantastic dancers. They had such good rhythm."

At just that moment, God sent Whitey around the corner.

"I can do the next best thing," I told her. "I can introduce you to one of the band members. He's standing right here."

I introduced them. They chatted for a while and then she said, "I'm so tired. I must sit down."

Whitey, being the polite man he was, accompanied her as she slowly walked into the USO canteen. Sylvia sat down, exhausted.

They visited for about ten or fifteen minutes. Then, Whitey stood and asked her, "Ma'am, may I have this dance?"

"What?" she asked, startled.

"May I have this dance?" he repeated.

"But there's no music," she pointed out.

"That's okay," he said, as he put her hand in his. He hummed one of the band's old tunes as he gently danced her around the floor.

It was very short and, with a final twirl, Whitey said, "Thank you for this dance."

Tears streamed down her cheeks. She rallied physically for a while, but the disease claimed her life a few months later. But Whitey helped one of her dreams come true.

That was Whitey. He was always the entertainer and loved the women. He passed away in California, but his memories are preserved forever at the museum.

Growing Awareness through Activities

We tried to increase awareness of the museum through participation in parades and displays at the Southwest Washington Fair. It seemed to work very well.

We displayed military photos and artifacts each year in a booth at the fair, starting in 1997.

We erected a display at the Washington State VFW convention in the summer of 2001 and we attended reunions of military groups.

We drove military vehicles in many community parades each year—Summerfest in Centralia and Pe Ell's Fourth of July, Christmas in Chehalis, Cheese Days in Toledo, Egg Day in Winlock, Independence Parade in Oakville, Swede Day in Rochester, Pioneer Days in Tenino, Funtime Festival in Napavine, Loggers Jubilee in Morton, and May Day in Vader.

For a few years, we even participated in parades in Olympia, as well as Loyalty Day in Long Beach, Washington, and local Memorial Day processions.

For the Chehalis Christmas Parade one year, we pulled a military trailer depicting A Soldier's Christmas with Korean War veterans wearing ponchos in the artificial snow, huddled over a small fire in a bucket, drinking coffee from canteen cups beside a scraggly tree decorated with beer cans, popcorn, and cut-out stars. It looked very realistic. Halfway through the parade, the wood in the bucket burst into flames, shooting fire in the air. The guys in the trailer threw coffee on the blaze, creating a very comical scene.

A Soldier's Christmas depicted in this December 2, 2000, parade float featuring Woody Schabell, Dave Dralle, Don Masterman, and John Blanchard. "A Soldier's Christmas" won first place in the parade.

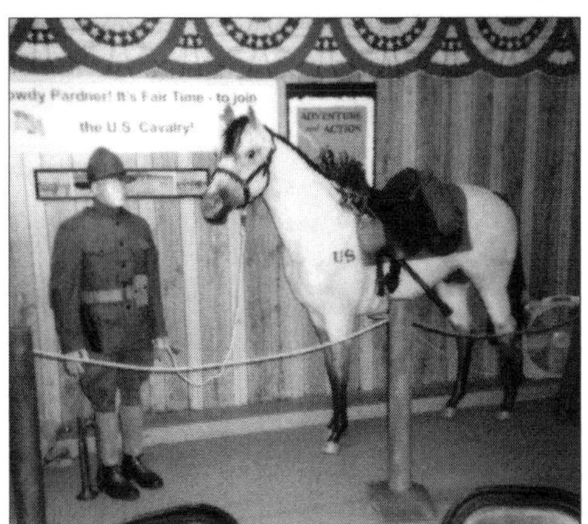

The 2000 Southwest Washington Fair booth featured the museum's military vehicles. Displayed above is a 1943 Ford GPW Jeep. At left, the 2005 Southwest Washington Fair booth featured a U.S. cavalry display with Veterans Memorial Museum icons Bart and Bucky. Below, Lee Grimes and Dale Ingle setting up for the 2004 Southwest Washington Fair booth featuring a Wall of Honor.

We won first place. We always seemed to win trophies for something. But we had an advantage: We were honoring the veterans.

Another time, our Christmas Parade theme was Rocking Around the Christmas Tree. We decorated the trailer with older veterans sitting in rocking chairs around a Christmas tree, rocking with children on their laps and at their feet, sharing stories. We received a grand prize for that one.

On another float, we erected a cross and veterans in uniform from the Civil War through the current conflict kneeled beside it, a hand on the shoulder of the man before him, representing the sacrifices of our military through the centuries. That float took another first-place prize.

We held days to recognize veterans from military conflicts—the WWII dinner dance, Korean War Remembrance Day, Vietnam Veteran Remembrance Day.

On July 24, 1999, the keynote speaker at the Second Annual Korean War Veterans Recognition Day was Wayne Galvin, who served from 1948 to 1952 in Japan and Korea as a crypto specialist in the Army Security Agency, a part of the Army Intelligence Division.

Wayne Galvin, U.S. Army Security Agency, speaks at the Second Annual Korean War Era Veterans Recognition Day.

He shared how much the public's indifference over the "police action" hurt returning veterans.

"When people are shooting lead at you and you are shooting lead at them and people are dying around you, it's a war," he told the nearly ninety people attending the event.

Galvin also spoke at the first-ever Cold War/Other Conflicts Day on August 24, 2000.

On September 18, 1999, we held our first-ever POW/MIA Remembrance Day at Borst Park, where Civil War re-enactors engaged in a mock battle in the wooded park. Smoke filtering through the trees made the performance more realistic. The museum honored more than fifty former POWs.

Guest speaker Robert Wheeler, who now lives in Napavine, shared his experiences as a child imprisoned in the Philippines during WWII. The 11th Airborne Division, "angels that fell from the sky," liberated the prison camp.

Keynote speaker Maurice Sharp of University Place, Washington, told of his years as a prisoner during the Korean War.

"The real heroes are those who did not return to enjoy the freedoms they fought so hard to preserve," he said.

During our early POW/MIA Remembrance Days, we formed a Walk of Honor for the ex-POWs and family members of the MIAs. At

The POW-MIA "Walk of Honor" ceremony in 2002.

least twenty veterans in their uniforms from all service branches and all eras formed two lines facing inward with a walkway between them. We read the names of each POW in attendance and each family member representing a POW or MIA and they would walk through the row flanked by uniformed veterans. Each veteran saluted them as they walked by. Many tears were shed by all and it was a very touching way to honor them for their tremendous sacrifice.

The following year, in September 2000, the keynote speaker was Bryce Lilly of Bothell, Washington, a survivor of the Bataan Death March. He described the sixty-mile march to Camp O'Donnell, which took five days and claimed the lives of approximately 10,000 Filipino and American soldiers.

Ex-POW Bryce Lilly, speaker at the POW-MIA Day September 16, 2000.

"Every ten or twelve steps, we were stepping over a body," said Lilly, who described himself as physically in good shape after boxing in the military and playing football and baseball.

Within three months of his incarceration,

his weight dropped from 185 to seventy pounds. He also buried many dead soldiers. To survive, he took one day at a time during his grueling three and a half years of imprisonment. He was working as a slave laborer in a Japanese steel mill when the war ended.

"After I was liberated, I weighed 190 in less than a month," he said. "I was eating six meals a day and making sandwiches in between."

His father died while he was overseas.

Another speaker was Gordon "Gordy" Clark, a former prisoner of war in Europe, who shared a story about his Merchant Marine uncle captured at Guadalcanal after his ship was torpedoed. He refused to work as a slave laborer and the Japanese killed him.

One of our special volunteer participants at several of our POW/MIA Remembrance Days was Harvey Rabbitt. Harvey is a wonderful Christian man with a very interesting background. He is a full-blooded Chippewa Indian, an ordained minister in the Assembly of God Church, and a twenty-year retired staff sergeant with the United State Marine Corps with two tours in Vietnam. Harvey would dress in his full Native American chief's regalia and give either the invocation or the meaning of the POW/MIA setting in his native tongue. I would read the English interpretation. Hearing a language that is almost forgotten would send chills up my spine! It was always very special when Harvey graced our programs with his participation.

We asked Harvey if he would like to carry the American flag in our parades; he gladly accepted. Wearing his Marine Corps uniform, he led the museum's parade entry as we walked along many Western Washington streets. If someone failed to pay proper respect as the flag passed by, Harvey became very upset, not during the parade but later he expressed his disappointment, saying that Americans have lost the proper respect for the U.S. flag.

I recall the first time I met Harvey. The museum had participated several years in the summer parade for the Oregon Trail Days in Tenino, Washington. I noticed a Native American always standing and saluting as we drove past him. I was introduced to him later and invited him to join us in our next parade. He said he would think about it but probably would not be available. Realizing he was a Vietnam veteran, I understood his reluctance. On our next parade date, much to my surprise, Harvey showed up in his Class A Marine Corps uniform, a bit tight around the seams but

SSGT Harvey Rabbitt, USMC (retired), above, during the Vietnam Traveling Wall visit in 2007. Below, SSGT Harvey Rabbitt, Chippewa Nation, served as chaplain on Korean War Era and POW-MIA Remembrance Day in 2004. He spoke in his native tongue.

it still fit. Harvey rode in the back of our Army deuce-and-a-half truck, behind the cab with Navy retiree Dick Shaver on the other side. After the parade, Harvey walked over to me, very emotional, and said, "Thank you. I had my Welcome Home parade today." Ever since that day, Harvey has been a strong supporter of the Veterans Memorial Museum.

Our guest speaker at the Fourth Annual Vietnam Veterans Remembrance Day in June 2001 was retired Lt. Col. Patti Hendrix, who served two tours in Vietnam as a field hospital nurse with the 85th Semi-Mobile Army Surgical Hospital at Phu Bai. She and her husband lived in Arlington, Washington, north of Seattle. Her riveting presentation focused on her lifelong memories of the wounded men who came through the battlefield hospitals, day in and day out.

After her presentation, we invited veterans to come forward and give their names, units of service, and the years they served in Vietnam. Sixty or so men walked forward, one at a time, and each one saluted the colonel. I don't think there was a dry eye among any of them. Many walked over to give her a hug for all the nurses who served.

Randy Pennington of Winlock, who served with the 101st Airborne, stood and told about his trip to the Phu Bai field hospital, where his friend, Sgt. Ken Perry, died. A nurse at the hospital comforted him with a hug; he believed Lt. Col. Hendrix was that nurse. Tears flowed freely as he shared his memories.

Then he started reading a poem he had written about war dogs.

War Dogs of Vietnam

Gather round me people, there is something I must say,
About some "Combat Soldiers" in a war so far away.
It was a time now near forgotten, in a land torn with strife,
They were called and did serve, and many gave up their life.

These "Troops" were very special, the best of the Elite.
You ask "What made them so special?"—they walked on all four feet.
Yes I am talking of the "War Dogs," as they have since been called,
They served and died in Vietnam, but their names are on no wall.

Randy Pennington reading his poem "War Dogs of Vietnam" at Vietnam Veterans Day in 2001.

Together with their partner they moved with stealth and skill,
And struck fear in the minds of the enemy,
who paid bounty to have them killed.
Some may have walked a sentry post, or down a jungle trail did go
Or at some distant air base, alerted to their foe.

So easy they could hear the wind, singing on a taut trip wire,
Or smell a "Zappers" satchel, before it became a deadly fire.
They would alert to a hidden enemy, at perhaps a 100 yards,
For us this was impossible, for them not even hard.

Their feats were so amazing, in the service that they gave,
And we will never know how many GI lives they saved.
They did so not for money, not for glory nor for fame,
But purely for devotion, a handler's love is why they came.

You say you never heard of them, so how do I know this is true?
For it seems so unbelievable, these things I say to you.
I tell you now, it was real, these things that came to be,
For I too was in the jungle, was a "Grunt" back then you see.

Yes I have seen and heard first hand, of these things that I do tell,
And with them shared brief encounters, in that steamy tropic hell.
Perhaps even mine could be a life that they did save
And I shall always be grateful for the service that they gave.

I know they are all gone now, time has passed beyond their years,
But sometimes I hear a dog bark, a memory returns with some tears
For they are but a memory, of a time long, long ago,
And there's a special place for these K-9s I have told to you.

"No greater love has a man, than to give up his life for his brother"
And so it must be, for these dogs that died saving others
And when I too shall cross over, to the place of Peace and Calm,
I will put my arms around their necks and say
"Thank You" to the War Dogs of Vietnam.

—Copyright ©
Randy S. Pennington

Nearby, a dog began to bark.

Patti Hendrix met her husband, John, a chopper pilot, at the hospital and six months later they married in Vietnam. They wrote a book called *To Have and To Hold: Love Formed Under Fire.* How they could find love in such a hideous place is amazing.

Her husband spoke at the Vietnam Veterans Remembrance Day in 2002. At that time, Randy Pennington read another poem, one he had written about the combat nurses, inspired by his meeting with Patti Hendrix the previous year. He called it "Reunion with an Angel." He had hoped Patti would attend with her husband, but she had another engagement. After Randy read the poem publicly, John Hendrix called his wife and Randy read the poem to her over the phone. Both were crying by the time he finished. John and Patti had been married for thirty-five years when John died in 2006.

Patti Hendrix, guest speaker, Vietnam Veterans Day in 2001.

REUNION WITH AN ANGEL

I once hugged an angel,
Although her wings could not be seen,
Just the same she was an angel,
And she was dressed in Army Green.

When first I did see her,
She was standing across the way,
With some "old soldiers,"
'Twas a "reunion" you might say.

A bunch of us "old soldiers"
Had gathered once again,
But on this day an "Angel" came,
To walk among us men.

She had come to talk to us,
Her story she would tell,
And I wondered if she knew,
She brought heaven into hell.

As she spoke of caring for the wounded,
Tears did fill her eyes,
She had worked in the hospital,
At a place called Phu Bai.

This name was not strange to me,
A nurse there once I knew,
I had been a "Screaming Eagle"
And had been at Phu Bai too.

My thoughts drifted back in time,
To a wounded friend with death so near,
And the rotors of a "Huey,"
Once again I seemed to hear.

I could see the "Dustoff"
As it rose into the air
And whisked my friend to Phu Bai,
They had the best of care.

When there too I was taken,
I learned God called my friend home.
I sank in deep despair
And I felt so all alone.

A nurse came over to me,
Said he is at peace above,
And she put her arms around me
And I drew strength out of her love!

When she turned and walked away,
I made a solemn vow,
I would return that hug someday,
Not knowing when or how.

My mind then brought me back,
To hear this nurse's closing words.

Could this be that same nurse?
Please God let it be her.

Then a soft voice inside me said
That she already knew,
If I returned this hug to her,
I'd be hugging all the nurses too.

Slowly then a line formed,
With each and every man,
Each waiting to tell her "Thank You"
And to shake her hand.

I said a silent prayer,
While I did also wait
That God would help her understand,
Why I returned this hug so late.
When face to face we came,
I said a handshake would not do,
And then I told her
"Patti, I must return something to you."

I put my arms around her,
The IOU was paid,
Fulfillment of a promise,
To a nurse long ago I made.

And, then she too embraced me,
And I knew the slate had been wiped clean.
My debt was finally paid in full,
And accepted by an angel,
An Angel dressed in Army Green.

Dedicated to Patti Hendrix and all the Vietnam nurses, in memory of my friend, Sgt. Ken Perry (panel 02w, line 83, Vietnam Memorial)

—Copyright © Randy Pennington

Glenn Miller Band trumpet player getting "his dome" dusted before TV filming of his WWII service, while below Lee Grimes is at left with WWI, U.S. Navy veteran Lawrence T. Dorsey, age 103, on November 11, 2002.

Pastor Allen Hull and Larry Blake cheering on newly activated and deployed Army National Guard.

We always assisted the Chehalis and Centralia Veterans of Foreign Wars and American Legion groups on Veterans Day and Memorial Day.

On Veterans Day, we participated often in a ceremony at St. Martin's University in Lacey, Washington, providing mannequins, flags, or making a presentation.

We held an annual appreciation picnic for our thirty to sixty volunteers, and the Polka Dots once again took the stage, with Barb on accordion, Loren on banjo, and me on the tuba.

KOMO-TV from Seattle featured one of our museum displays—that of Whitey Thomas, who performed with the Glen Miller Band. I'll never forget how they dusted powder on his bald head so that it wouldn't shine during the filming. He played his trumpet, as well as the trombone.

On Veterans Day 2002, we had our third WWI visitor at the museum.

Lawrence T. Dorsey, a 103-year-old U.S. Navy WWI veteran from Vancouver, Washington, was living in a nursing home. Employees from the home brought him and a busload of veterans to the museum for our Veterans Day ceremony. We presented him with a Remembrance Medallion.

And in November 2002, when our local 81st National Guard Brigade was activated, we stood in the street and waved flags and "Support our Troops" signs as our local men and women left for the war in the Middle East.

Honored by the DAR

I received a special honor March 24, 2001, when the Daughters of the American Revolution bestowed the national Medal of Honor on me at the 100th Washington State Society Convention in Seattle. The medal is the highest honor the national organization gives an American citizen exemplifying its objective "to promote knowledge, loyalty, and love of country." The organization bestows only one such medal in the United States each year. Other recipients have included presidents, generals, and astronauts.

"Mr. Grimes, himself, is not a veteran, rather he is a Godly and patriotic citizen pursuing a mission to preserve much that was in danger of being lost," said Harriet Rounsely, chapter regent.

A letter from the national DAR described my "incredible achievement in the cause of honoring/remembering the veterans to whom we owe our liberty."

The DAR contacted my wife about submitting my name. I was selected as winner at the state and national levels. I was pretty thrilled. They did a local presentation, too.

"I'm extremely honored to receive this award," I said at the time. "Although it was given to me as an individual, I share this with all veterans who have served this nation, for it is (to) their sacrifices and memories that we dedicate this museum."

Running out of Room

We provided countless tours to schools, Scouts, and veterans groups.

We soon found ourselves running out of room. We had no more storage for artifacts. We couldn't store our equipment anywhere. We held programs outside in a courtyard.

If more than twenty people arrived for a tour, it was too crowded inside. The aisles were only thirty inches wide, with display cases on either side. It was almost uncomfortable to take a tour through the museum, especially for people in wheelchairs.

We had outgrown the building, so the board of directors decided to look into expanding the museum.

We looked for an existing building with better parking. We searched in Centralia. We looked in Chehalis. We considered the old Centralia sewage treatment plant, but hesitated because it had flooded in the past. It wasn't free; we'd have to pay rent as we were then.

We looked at a metal building behind the Twin Cities Auction, but it wasn't very visible.

Then we explored the option of building a new museum.

One day Chehalis Mayor Bob Spahr called me.

"If we lease you property next to the freeway, would you consider moving over here?" he asked. His father, Emil Spahr, had served in the Army Air Corps on the island of Saipan during WWII.

One of our highest priorities was freeway visibility to increase traffic. The city owned two and a half acres beside Interstate 5 near the Chehalis-Centralia Railroad and Museum. The Chehalis City Council offered to lease the land to us for one dollar a year for 120 years. Council members understood what the museum was and shared our vision to expand.

Mayor Spahr said to me, "Make sure you come with open eyes!"

I looked at the property with the mayor. We discovered an absolute mess, a dumping ground for contractors and others who left cables, boards, and other debris amid the overgrown jungle of blackberries.

I could see beyond the mess. I looked at the freeway and I looked at the property.

"Yeah, we'll take her," I said.

Later, Centralia city officials asked if we'd be receptive to staying in Centralia if they bought property near the freeway and leased it to us for a dollar a year. I said yes, since we had started in Centralia.

But several months passed and we never heard anything more. We signed the lease with Chehalis October 3, 2000.

Now we had a place to build, but we needed to raise money for construction.

Norm Pfaff, a local architect, volunteered to draw the plans for our new building. He developed plans for a beautiful $1.8 million museum.

WWII dinner/dance veterans, from left, Loren Estep, Gene Cole, Ken Grant, Ken Robinette, Harry Estep, and Jack Crocker. "Looks like they have been on liberty."

We held fundraisers. We sold life memberships. We asked for donations.

We sold one-hundred-dollar memorial tiles for what would become our Wall of Honor, each white tile bearing in black lettering the name of a veteran and the branch and years of military service.

We collected money for the new building at the WWII dinner dance, a fun evening where veterans and their spouses dressed in 1940s garb, danced the jitterbug, and participated in contests to identify the oldest, best dressed, and farthest traveled veterans. At its peak, more than four hundred people attended the dinner and dance, packing the Centralia Eagles hall.

Barb was responsible for writing the only grant we have received; the Ben Cheney Foundation offered $5,000 when we started the museum in 1997 and later gave us a $35,000 grant.

We hired a grant writer to secure grants. We hired three grant writers over four years and never got a dime.

Above, George Gill of George Gill Construction while below is a shot of the first dirt being moved for the new museum.

The money trickled in. Something told me that it just wasn't right. I attended a home and garden show at the fairgrounds, where I found a Metal Mill exhibit. I saw businesses that erected attractive metal buildings. I didn't think metal buildings could look so good.

I asked Mark Bolender of Silver Creek, who owned the Metal Mill, to put together a design for us. A few weeks later, he provided a similar design that cost $600,000 less while almost twice the size. The price tag for the metal museum was $1.2 million.

We addressed issues of preserving the artifacts properly in a metal building. We needed adequate insulation, heat pumps that regulated humidity and ensured that temperatures never varied more than five degrees.

The hard part was returning to Norm Pfaff. I told him we appreciated all his hard work but decided to go with a different design. I hated to hurt him.

But when we accepted the $1.2 million plans, the money started rolling in. It was almost like God said you just need something that's basic, not fancy.

Local Rotary clubs held a tri-club auction every year, donating the proceeds to a nonprofit organization. The Rotary selected the museum as its recipient in March 2002 and the auction raised $31,659. That was almost enough to clear and fill the land, which was estimated to cost $35,000 through George Gill Construction of Centralia, which was virtually a gift.

The Altrusa group donated $3,000 to the museum endowment fund, provided in three annual checks. We raised several thousand dollars through raffles, breakfasts, garage sales, and other fundraisers, which all received tremendous support from the surrounding area.

As our building fund grew, we broke ground, figuring that as people saw something happening, they would donate even more. We started the fill work after the Rotary auction in May 2002. We knew that the area had flooded in the past, so we placed fill dirt to raise it above the floodplain. The code required us to build one foot higher than the highest point of flooding, which at that time had occurred in 1996.

But to be sure, we built two feet higher than we were required to build, which was three feet above the 1996 flood levels. We should have been safe there.

Although we had only $32,000, we told George Gill to go ahead with the work. When he presented me with a bill for $41,000, I said,

"George, all I have is $32,000 at the moment. I know it's a gift that you're giving us. I'll have the rest of it shortly. Bear with me for a little while."

I apologized and felt bad that we couldn't pay him for the work he'd done. We still owed him $9,000.

Chapter Six:

Melvin and Katherine Nesteby

IN THE SUMMER OF 1998, BARB AND I drove to North Dakota to visit family members and friends. We were driving our personal van that we had painted green with the words Veterans Memorial Museum on the side. It was another way to promote the museum. We bought the materials and Ken Rollins, a Vietnam veteran, painted it for us at no charge.

When we returned over White Pass on Highway 12, we saw a disabled vehicle on the side of the road, an older couple beside the car with its hood up. We drove past, and I said to Barb, "We're going back to see if we can help that older couple." So we found the next turnout and headed back to them. I got out, introduced myself, and asked if I could help.

This older gentleman said the car just quit.

Now I can change spark plugs and oil, but I'm no mechanic. But I told him I'd take a look under the hood. It was an older car, but nothing seemed out of place. I checked the spark plug wires, looked at the coil lead, shook the battery cables, and then prayed. Okay, Lord, let's get these folks going.

Leaning my head around the hood, I said, "Go ahead and give her a try."

He turned the key and the engine started up immediately. He couldn't get over the fact that I got his car going. It wasn't me; we had

Ken Rollins, Vietnam veteran, and Lee Grimes with the newly painted museum van completed in Ken's shop.

some help from above. We said we'd follow them as far as Centralia. There we would pull ahead of them and they could stop by our house where we all could enjoy a drink and rest for a bit before they moved on.

The couple—Melvin and Katherine Nesteby of Olympia—stopped for a bit and drank some water. We chatted a little. He asked about the van and I told him about my vision to start a museum to honor veterans. He told us briefly that he had served in the Army and became a prisoner of war. Then they took off.

In November 2003, the telephone at the museum rang.

"Is your name Lee Grimes?" an older man asked.

"Yes, sir," I responded.

"Are you the guy who stopped on the mountaintop a few years ago and helped an older couple?"

We had been raised to help people along the side of the road. It was just something we were taught to do in North Dakota, so I was a bit at a loss. I had to stop and think.

"Yeah, I remember stopping and helping someone," I said.

"And your wife's name was Barbara," he said. "You drove a green van with Army stars on it and you shared your dream of the museum to honor veterans."

"That would be me," I affirmed.

"I'm glad I was able to find you," he said. "Would you come up to my apartment? I have a lot of military things here that I would like to donate to the museum."

"Sure," I said. I jotted down the address and set a time.

Mel and Katherine Nesteby at the POW-MIA Remembrance Day in 2004.

I took Dale Ingle, one of our board members, with me and met Melvin and Katherine Nesteby again. When we entered the apartment, we saw that he had all of his military and war memorabilia neatly laid out on the floor with notes on each item. He kept everything in plastic wrap to protect it.

The Nestebys wanted to find a place to preserve his memorabilia of war and faith and, after looking for twenty years, agreed to give it to the Veterans Memorial Museum.

Mel began to share some of the stories of his days in the service and as a POW. We sat there for an hour or so. We just loved listening to his stories.

We gathered his things together and as we headed for the door, he stopped us.

"Oh, by the way, I nearly forgot this," Melvin said, reaching into his pocket. He pulled out a check and handed it to me.

"Take $2,000 of this and put it in your operating fund and the rest of it can go to your new building fund," he said. We hadn't even mentioned our need to finance the new museum.

I looked at the check. It was for $11,000. We needed $9,000 for George Gill Construction and God provided the money through Melvin and Katherine Nesteby, a Christian couple. Praise God! We thanked them profusely.

"This is exactly what we needed," I told them. "I feel God is guiding our paths."

"I feel the same way, too," he said.

One of the items he gave us was a Bible. But it wasn't just any Bible.

We returned to the museum, wrote a letter to thank them for their donations, and decided to recognize him by putting up his display immediately. We displayed Mel's twenty medals, a letter of appreciation from the Korean president, and a black-and-white photograph of him in Tokyo. The display included a picture of Jesus from the couple's living room and a sample of Katherine's embroidery.

But front and center in the display case was a rack holding the tattered, black-covered New Testament.

Around Christmas 2003, I received a call from Mel. He asked if Dale and Linda Ingle and Barb and I could visit for dinner and fellowship. We arranged a date and time and took them to dinner at the Red Lobster in Olympia. They invited us back to their apartment for some fellowship and dessert.

Mel shared more stories about his days in the military and life as a POW. Then he changed the subject.

"My wife and I have been thinking," Mel said. "We've been thinking you need money for the endowment fund to keep the new museum going. I will not sign any documents—my word is my honor, my handshake will seal our deal—so I will shake your hand and my wife and I today pledge to the museum $50,000."

I felt overwhelmed.

He asked that the donation be anonymous so they didn't have people banging on their doors asking for money.

"We can certainly grant that request," I said.

Within a week or two, we received a check from them for $50,000. We deposited it into our endowment fund.

In February 2004, we asked if he would like to come down to dedicate his display case. We set the date and invited *The Chronicle* newspaper in Centralia to cover the event.

The day before the dedication, he called. "I've got a request," he said. "Last night when I was lying in bed, I had this real urge to rededicate the prayer I had before I went off to battle and was captured."

"The evening before the battle, the chaplain came around and asked if anyone would like to have a prayer before going into battle. My hand immediately shot up and I said, 'Yes, sir, I do.' The chaplain placed his hand on my head and offered a prayer for my safety in the coming battle."

Pastor Allen Hull, Mel Nesteby, and Lee Grimes admiring Mel's display at his prayer dedication.

So I asked retired Baptist Pastor Allen Hull of Napavine if he could pray over Mr. Nesteby. He was happy to do it. He put on his Army uniform and the museum provided a black chaplain's WWII stole emblazoned with a cross.

When Melvin Nesteby arrived at the museum, the first thing he wanted was that prayer of dedication.

We folded an Army blanket and placed it on the concrete floor. He knelt on the blanket and Pastor Hull opened his Bible, placed his hand on him, and offered prayers for his life, safe return, and service to our country.

"Thank you for the strength Mel received in his ordeal and for the hundreds who went to see eternity holding this Bible," Hull prayed.

Everybody grew a bit teary-eyed watching the rededicated prayer. We helped the tall Norwegian to his feet and then reporter Brian Mittge interviewed him and wrote a story for *The Chronicle* under the headline "From Bataan to Centralia."

The story spoke about his experiences as a POW in the Philippines during WWII, picking through rice for tiny white protein-rich worms he auctioned off to fellow prisoners. Mel described the beatings and torture, injuries, and starvation.

He also told about the pocket New Testament he received after joining the Army in Minnesota. He had attended a small country church and the Gideons were passing out pocket Bibles. Mel immediately accepted his and carried it with him to the Philippines.

When Mel was first captured, Japanese guards came around with small ditty bags and took all the personal belongings of the soldiers—wallets, rings, watches, and so on. Mel tried to hide his Bible—the one thing he wanted to keep—but to no avail. It was gone.

Eighteen months later, in another POW camp many miles away where he had been moved, Mel contracted malaria. Lying in bed, delirious with the fever, he recalled someone standing beside his bed one day, saying "I believe I have something that is yours." He pressed something into his hand.

A few days later when the fever broke, Mel felt this object in his hand. He looked at it and saw his lost Bible! Mel said, "I truly believe an angel brought my Bible back to me that day."

He learned it had been kept in the "Zero Ward," where American soldiers were sent to die. The Bible was given to hundreds of young men as they lay dying, offering spiritual comfort as they left this world for another.

Serving on the front lines in April 1942, Mel was injured and hobbled on bamboo crutches as the Bataan Death March began, but the injured were falling behind and feared they'd be shot. For some unknown reason, a Japanese guard took pity on some of them and ordered Mel and the other injured soldiers back to a hospital.

After being a POW, Mel served in Korea and retired from the Army in 1962.

After the ceremony dedicating his display case, Mel pulled me aside. "May my wife and I talk to you in private?" he asked.

"Sure," I responded.

We walked into the library and shut the door.

"My wife and I have been thinking that we made a mistake," he said. "We put a stipulation on those funds, that they be used for your endowment fund, but we now realize you must build your building first, so we withdraw that stipulation.

"You may use one dollar of it or all of it for the building fund, and we will reimburse you," he continued. "Oh, the heck with it, use the $50,000 for the building fund and we pledge to you today another $50,000."

My mouth dropped open. Barb started crying.

"That won't come in one check, but it will come over the next few months," Mel said. "We have some investments."

The money arrived over the next several months. It seemed like just when we were running out of money, here came another check for $10,000 or $15,000.

Mel and Katherine visited when the shell of the new building was erected. There was no interior wall structure whatsoever. We showed them where things would be—the offices, gift shop, gallery, and storage areas. They seemed pleased and prepared to leave but stopped at the door. Mel pulled out another check.

"Here's just a little bit more for the building," he said. It was $10,000.

Altogether, we received $121,000 from this wonderful couple.

As he was leaving, Mel reached for the door, stopped, and turned around.

"Do you remember that meeting on the mountaintop so many years ago?" he asked. "You know, God had a plan for both of us.

"What you have done for me to keep my memory alive is more than this money will ever do for you."

I was thinking just the opposite. What they did for this museum can never be repaid. He wanted the donations to be anonymous. He asked only that fifteen or twenty family members and friends be given lifetime memberships to the museum. That's all he requested.

(Several years later, when the U.S. Army Museum in Washington, D.C., established a national museum, Mel requested that his items be placed there. We reluctantly obliged.)

Chapter Seven:

Raising Money and Breaking Ground

WE HELD MORE FUNDRAISERS and our coffers began to grow.

John Lee and his wife, Sarah, hosted a benefit breakfast for us at their downtown Centralia restaurant, Sarah's Garden Café. He is a South Korean national who served in the Republic of Korea (ROK) Marine Corps during the 1950s and early 1960s.

Sarah's parents lived in North Korea and, during the Korean War as the communists moved south, her family fled to South Korea. Her father had earlier traveled to South Korea to learn about the political situation between the two countries and determine whether he should move his family south. When the war broke out, he did not return but sent a message to Sarah's mother, telling her to bring the family to South Korea where he was staying. Sarah was just a small child as her mother and grandmother traveled along the back roads, fleeing literally for their lives. If they were caught, they would either be executed or forced to return north. As they traveled, when they met American forces, GIs would give them C rations. Her mother opened the cans of meat with the thick layers of grease or fat congealed on top. Sarah was fed the fat as baby food. Today, she says, "Thank you, American GI!" The family was reunited at a river near Pusan.

At left, John Lee with "Pvt. Sad Sack" at a fundraising breakfast January 8, 2004, while below on the same day are John and Sarah Lee with Bill Logan in front and, in back, from left, Mrs. Choi, Pastor Choi, John Lee, Lee Grimes, Sarah Lee, Young A. Ko, and Dale Ingle.

It should be noted that Sarah's grandmother carried the family's prized possession on her back during the entire trip on foot—a Singer sewing machine.

Both John and Sarah had immigrated to the United States where they met and were married.

They bought a house in Chehalis, heard we were raising money for the museum, and wanted to help.

"Why not have a breakfast and all the money we bring in goes to the museum?" he asked. He's a jovial, outgoing Christian man.

We held the breakfast January 8, 2004, at Sarah's Garden Café in Centralia, which is no longer there.

Dale Ingle, Bill Logan, and I helped by greeting folks, serving food, cleaning tables, and cooking. Clown that I am, I donned a big cook's stove hat bearing the words "Pvt. Sad Sack" as I helped in the kitchen.

I'm not sure how much money we raised, perhaps a thousand dollars. But the idea counted more than anything, the fact that a Korean couple felt so appreciative of what American GIs had done for their family.

Shortly after the breakfast, John invited me to speak to the Republic of Korea Marine Corps Association, made up of Korean veterans living in America. The meeting took place at his house. We enjoyed a wonderful steak dinner and Asian food. Most of the fifteen or so guys spoke very little English, but a couple of the younger men were very fluent. They interpreted what I said and the comments from the Koreans, who were gracious and polite.

They asked if they could put a tile on the Wall of Honor for the Korean marines and I said sure. They settled on two tiles that read, "ROK Marine Corps League, Once a Marine, Always a Marine," and "ROK Marine Corps, Semper Fi."

We raised money through raffles, benefits, and the sale of life memberships. Our biggest fundraiser by far was the sale of ceramic tiles for the Wall of Honor, which at one hundred dollars each raised $160,000. Tom Alderson at Printwares, or Awards West, engraved tiles for us with a laser.

We've raised another $40,000 through the tile program since the construction and that money goes into a perpetual fund that earns interest for the operating budget.

We figured our annual budget would be $120,000, so we needed to raise $10,000 a month. That's hard to do when all you're selling is five-dollar admissions, plus T-shirts and hats.

We held a groundbreaking ceremony on September 26, 2003, with flags flying and a large picture showing what the new museum building would look like. We had obtained a black-and-white picture from The Metal Mill and a Centralia College student Tyler Davis colorized it, inserting trees and landscaping.

We laid out thirteen shovels and invited local dignitaries, veterans, and friends to attend. Approximately two hundred people showed up. I gave a short speech about seeing our vision come true. We invited the participants to grab a shovel and on cue turn the dirt. Those first thirteen people were Bonnie Canaday, Bob Spahr, Eric Johnson, Wayne Galvin, George Gill, Todd Mason, Rose Bowman, Ed Herold, Mike Austin, Dave Mundine, John Hanson, Rev. Darcy Fast, and Mark Bolender. We then invited anyone else who wanted to turn a shovel full of dirt to do so. More than forty people responded so we repeated the ceremony several times. This museum always has been, is, and forever will be the people's museum.

The Chehalis City Council voted to change the name of the street from Thomas Street to Veterans Way and presented us with the red, white, and blue street sign.

Initial "turning of the soil" by the first thirteen.

Mayor Bob Spahr and Lee Grimes hold a sign for the newly named street "Veterans Way" while Tim Grochowski, Chehalis Public Works director, stands behind Lee. Below, from left, are Dave Mundine, structural contractor, Mark Bolender, general contractor, and Lee Grimes.

Mark Bolender served as project manager and general contractor and Dave Mundine was structural contractor.

Shortly after the groundbreaking, on October 20, 2003, we received a check from the state of Washington's Economic Development Department for tourism-related buildings. The amount: $225,000.

I had heard a veteran say we were included in the state budget, but that was news to me. I called our 20th District lawmakers.

"Yeah, I put that in the budget," said Rep. Richard DeBolt, a Republican from Chehalis. "It's a worthy cause, and all these other districts are getting money for this type of cause. The money's here, so I decided to put the museum in for it."

I filled out some paperwork. Richard told me that he saw the money as providing hands-on results, rather than just funding another study somewhere. "At least here, you can place your hands on it and see the results of it," Richard said.

One day during the fundraising frenzy, I received a letter from New Rochelle, New York, written by Marguerite Jasper, the WWII nurse I had interviewed. In the envelope I found three one-dollar bills. She said she had been clipping coupons and turning them in for cash. It took ten coupons to make a penny. She said, "This is all I can afford."

It was like the widow's mite from the Bible. She wasn't a widow, but she had worked hard for that money. Those three dollars meant as much to me as the $225,000.

Many people stepped forward to volunteer time, material, and services. We needed people to tie rebar and they volunteered. We needed equipment and Chehalis Rentals and United Rentals donated dozers and shovels. We needed operators and they arrived to help. Retired contractors showed up.

In November 2003, we probably received at least $300,000 of in-kind labor and donations. We poured one and a half acres of concrete November 3. The building itself is 20,500 square feet, compared with 3,500 square feet at the Main Street building in Centralia.

The steel shipment arrived November 24 and construction began in December.

By February 2004, we had the building enclosed. By the summer of 2004, we were working on the walls inside the building.

The steel skeleton of the new building in December 2003, above, and enclosed in February 2004, below.

It was hot and I was sweating heavily in eighty-degree heat, balancing on a sixteen-foot ladder to spread Sheetrock mud on the wall on the second level when I heard my name.

"Hey, Lee Grimes up there?"

I was thinking, *Don't bother me! I'm busy.* I didn't answer.

I heard the voice again. "Hey, Lee Grimes up there?"

"Yeah, I'm here," I responded, a trace of irritation in my voice.

"Come on down here," the man said. "I've got to talk to you."

"I'm pretty busy putting Sheetrock mud up," I said. "I'm covered head to toe with mud."

"I need to talk to you right now."

"Okay. I'll be down in a couple of minutes."

I trudged down the steps of the ladder and down the back steps to the main floor.

"I've just been over to the old museum," the man said. "Those tiles that you're selling. I want one of those tiles."

"Okay, no problem," I said. "That will be one hundred dollars."

He told me he wanted three tiles altogether, including one for his brother.

"Okay," I said. "That will be three hundred dollars."

"Can you write?" he asked me.

I was taken aback, a little irritated by then.

"Yes, sir, I can write."

"Can you read it?" he asked.

"Yes, sir, I can write legibly," I responded.

Gesturing, he told me, "Sit down here and write this check out for $25,000."

"Excuse me?" I said.

"What's the matter? Can't you hear?" he asked.

"No, sir, I heard. I just wanted to make sure I heard it right."

I wrote the check for $25,000 and he signed his name to it and headed out the door. He was Don Coleman, a Pearl Harbor survivor and Centralia businessman. He attended our grand opening and one of our Pearl Harbor events. He was a member of the museum, but not actively involved.

That day taught me a lesson: You always stop and take time for someone. God sent somebody my way that day and I almost turned my back on him.

Chet Landmark, drywall texturer bar none, enjoying his work.

I always make time for people now. I might have to think for a moment, but I take the time.

We had the inside walls erected, mudded and sanded, but we needed them textured. I wished I knew somebody who could do this. One of our members, Walt Olson, said he used to know a guy who did that work.

I met the man, Chet Landmark, a drywaller from Tacoma, Washington, explained what we were doing, and asked if he would like to texture the walls for us.

He looked at the interior of the building.

"That's a lot of walls to texture," he said.

I acknowledged his statement was true.

"I wouldn't mind doing this for you," he said.

"Can you give me a bid on it?" I asked.

"I've got to drive all the way down from Tacoma with my equipment," he said. "How about one hundred dollars? For gas money."

I couldn't believe it.

"Well, gosh, if that's your offer, we certainly appreciate that."

We bought the bags of drywall powder, which he mixed into a cream. He brought hoses and guns and, because he was about six-foot-seven, he could spray the walls without using a ladder.

He completed the bottom floor first. I handed him an envelope with one hundred dollars.

"What's that?" he asked.

"This was our agreement," I told him.

"I don't want that," he said. "Where would we be without our veterans? This is the way I can contribute to them. When you get ready to do the upstairs, the price is the same."

It seemed that whenever we needed something, the good Lord just sent somebody our way. We were walking a blessed path.

On December 4, 2004, we received a check from the Ben B. Cheney Foundation for $35,000. Ben Cheney, who died in 1971, was a multimillionaire who earned his living in the timber industry. His foundation, established in 1955, started making grants in 1975 and, through 2008, had awarded 4,295 grants totaling $72.5 million.

Below, Don Masterman with his wife, Carolyn, on his final visit to the museum. Volunteer Donna Loucks explains the new library.

Out of more than a hundred foundations we investigated, they were the only one we applied to that gave us money. The others said the museum, while a nice project, didn't fit their mission. I grew so frustrated we decided, the heck with it. We'll do it ourselves. People say, "Just go out and get a grant," but it's not that easy.

We grew to know well so many wonderful volunteers.

One of them, Don Masterman, an Army veteran from Rochester, Washington, who drove Jeeps for us in parades and manned the front desk at the old museum, was diagnosed with cancer in early 2005. It spread rapidly through his body. His wife, Carolyn, also spent many hours volunteering at the museum, manning the front desk, carrying banners in the parades, cleaning, and doing other work. She told us Don wanted to see the museum before he died.

He arrived in a wheelchair and we gave him a tour of the building. The walls were painted, but we still had work to do. We showed him where the cabinets would be placed and the library. He sat there and smiled as we described what it would be like, with the display cabinets in place and the books lining library shelves. It was his final visit, but it reinforced us to know how much this place meant to people.

He wanted to visit the museum, even though he was on his deathbed.

It's a miracle that we raised $1.5 million to build this museum. But the greater miracles happen inside the museum, where God's presence embraces these wounded souls and provides healing to hurting hearts and guidance through life.

"Christmas Reindeer" Don Masterman, left, and Lee Grimes ready for the Christmas Parade. Korean War veteran Larry Campbell is in back.

Chapter Eight:

Building a Museum

Our contractors

The museum wouldn't be here today without the help of Dave Dralle, Dave Mundine, and Mark Bolender.

Mark, president and owner of The Metal Mill at Silver Creek, Washington, served as general contractor and project manager. He's also a Christian man and many times during the project, when I grew frustrated, Mark would tell me to calm down.

"Let's go over here and just have a prayer," he'd say. He would pray for me to slow down and let God do his work.

Dave Mundine of DM Construction in Chehalis served as structural contractor, overseeing the pouring of concrete and erection of the building's shell.

After completing the fill and passing the compaction inspection, we began digging the huge holes for concrete to support the main steel pillars and digging plumbing and electrical trenches and outer foundation forms. Once the electrical and plumbing lines were run, we laid rebar and more rebar and more rebar! Each piece of rebar that crisscrossed another had to be tied. We called for volunteers and so many came to do the backbreaking work, I didn't even know who many of them were. On November 13, 2004, the concrete trucks began to arrive at 5 a.m. and continued on a steady pace for fifteen and a half hours until 8:30 p.m.

Dave Dralle, volunteer contractor, moves dirt at the new building site, above. Below, the Moran Brothers Plumbing, Tim, left, and Fred, far right, exceptional plumbers, lay pipe to the final water cooler.

During this time frame, twenty-four trucks had arrived to deliver 252 yards of concrete. We now had a slab of nearly 25,000 square feet.

Dave Dralle, who served in the Marine Corps in the post-Korean War era, served as our volunteer contractor. For three years, he was here nearly every day. He had worked as a contractor in California before moving to Adna, Washington. He also offered us use of his backhoe and other heavy equipment. Dave put in the most volunteer time of anyone on this project.

Dave Dralle and I decided we could do all the interior work with volunteers. We had thirty to fifty people ready, willing, and able to help.

During the construction, friends told me I looked like death warmed over. I felt fine, but I did feel the stress of making sure everything was done. I was here every day. We did so much of the work ourselves. We spray painted, hammered nails, put up Sheetrock, taped and mudded the building. My only training came from remodeling projects at home.

Dave Dralle dug trenches, laid pipe, and oversaw jail inmates on the work crews.

We had probably two to four inmates here every day working on the construction, and probably as many as sixty altogether. After we opened, I noticed that these guys who had served time for unpaid tickets or drug violations or driving while intoxicated often stopped by the museum with family members or friends. I'd hear them say, "I helped build this place."

Dave treated them well, always providing them with donuts and cigarettes. Most of them were more than happy to work. Usually the jail supervisors didn't want inmates working two days in a row on the same project, because their girlfriends or friends could contact them or slip them some drugs. But when we found good workers, they would send them to the museum.

Inmates placed 95 percent of the 540 sheets of Sheetrock in the building. Each was four by twelve feet, five-eighths inches thick, weighing about 112 pounds. They were heavy. We gave the inmates the job of toting and putting up the Sheetrock that we screwed to the studs. I came along and slapped mud and tape on them. Then other volunteers sanded the joints and I put another coat of mud over it, filling in the concave part of the Sheetrock. We did that three times for each seam until it was two feet wide across and the joint was invisible. We hoisted sheets twenty feet off the ground to place them on the outer side of the upstairs wall.

Setting forms for the concrete footings, above, with Bill Logan holding the survey stick. Below, volunteers do the back-breaking job of tying thousands of feet of rebar. Allen Erickson and Al Hatton take a picture break.

Above, Loren Estep, Doss Champ and Bob Thornburg have a good time while working. Below are Frank DeAbreau, Jay Hall, and Jim Thompson, construction volunteers.

We saved tens of thousands of dollars by doing the work ourselves with the inmates' help.

I look around this building and I see people in every square inch—Art Williams, who sanded Sheetrock seams just after undergoing open-heart surgery; Ernie Graichen and Pat Swanson, who helped me cut and set all the molding; Wayne Galvin, who painted all the trim. Ernie is a woodworker, so he crafted the oak window frames at home. Palmer Millwork gave us a deal on staining all the doors. Bob Thornburg, a master builder, volunteered to build the stairwells, upstairs bathrooms, the elevator maintenance room, and the fireproofed elevator shaft to exact code specifications. He did the work in a few days when it would have taken us months. Bob served in the U.S. Army First Armored Division at the rank of SP4. Otis Installers put in the elevator. Frank DeAbreau and Jim Thompson cut and nailed studs together for walls.

A city inspector made sure we did everything by the book, counting the screws before we mudded. We hired certified contractors to do the plumbing and electrical work. Fred and Tim Moran of Moran Brothers did the plumbing and Travers Electric did the electrical work. Chehalis Sheet Metal installed the heating and air-conditioning system. Ed Weed and Darrel Gutsche laid the tile in both first-floor bathrooms.

From the ground up, I've almost become a part of the building. I know every nook and cranny, what's behind the walls and above the ceilings. We left mementos under the stairwells—little notes, coins, and dollar bills. We had tremendous fun doing this.

Although Dave Dralle is of German descent, Bill Logan and I are Scandinavian, so the three of us spoke with Norwegian accents and called each other by Scandinavian names—Hagar the Horrible (Dave), Sven Logangardsen (Bill), and Ole Bjornsen, which was my nickname.

We tried to keep everybody on an upbeat mode all the time. We didn't have many conflicts.

HOLDING EVENTS IN A SHELL OF A BUILDING

Even though the museum hadn't officially opened, we held a few events there before our grand opening.

In early June 2004, we held the Seventh Annual Vietnam Veterans Remembrance Day in the enclosed but unfinished building. We focused the program on War Dogs and their Handlers.

Guest speaker Randy Ransom of Shelton, Washington, served with the 48th Infantry Platoon Scout Dogs in Vietnam. Native American Dog Handler Lalo Valdez performed the lighting of the POW/MIA candle.

Many of the scout dogs were killed in action. When the United States pulled out of Vietnam, the government didn't allow handlers to take their dogs home to the States. Most of the canines were either euthanized or turned over to the South Vietnamese Army.

Randy was hesitant about presenting in front of several hundred people, but we encouraged him. He started to talk about his dog, Hasso.

"I never trained Hasso. Hasso trained me."

That's all he could say. Then he began to choke up. It was Hasso's second tour and Randy's first. At the time, Randy was OJT—on-the-job training. Nobody handling Hasso ever got a Purple Heart.

Randy stepped outside and another dog handler spoke instead. It was fine. Randy was speaking from the heart.

After the program ended, Randy approached me to apologize. He felt that he had failed.

"Heavens no!" I said. "You did the best you could; that was all we ever asked."

"I brought Hasso's harness with me," Randy said. "I want to donate it to the museum, but I just don't know if I can. I can still smell him on it. I've been sleeping with the harness the last ten nights."

"It would be an honor to have it," I told him. "But keep it. If it means that much, you need to keep it."

"But I can't keep it," Randy said. "Hasso is a veteran, too, and he needs to be in here amongst his comrades in arms."

He left the harness in our care. He asked only that he be allowed to come in once a year to treat the harness with bear grease. When he returned in December to treat the harness, he said, "I'm doing fine. I'll never let Hasso go. He lives here now and in my heart forever."

That same month, we held our WWII dinner dance where the main gallery was to be. We brought in tables and chairs from the Church of God, hired an eighteen-piece swing band called "The Sound of Swing," and enjoyed a dinner catered by Trina Gardepie.

Retired Lewis County Sheriff Bill Logan, a museum member, has never been bashful. He brought an unsigned check for $1,000 and announced that he would sign the check if another $1,000 could be collected in the big pickle jar he held in his hand. Cash and checks began waving throughout the crowd and after people passed the pickle jar around the room, more than $7,500 had been donated. Bill signed his check to bring the total to $8,500. Another museum member, Walt Olson, issued his challenge: If we could raise a total of $9,000 he would also sign a check for an additional $1,000. The pickle jar made its rounds again and another $800 was raised, bringing the total to more than $9,300. Walt signed his check and we had raised a total of $10,433! It's amazing what a pickle jar can do!

In September the museum was the site of the Seventh Annual Korean War and POW/MIA Remembrance Day.

In December, vandals once again broke out the front windows of the Main Street museum in Centralia. We realized it was a random act of violence, but still, to damage a place that honors veterans and their sacrifices boggles the mind. It was the second time we'd been vandalized at that location.

The first time occurred on Memorial Day weekend in 1999, when I received a call from Centralia police at 6 a.m. on a Saturday telling me someone had shattered a large pane of front window glass bearing the museum's logo—They Shall Not Be Forgotten.

MOVING INTO THE NEW MUSEUM

On January 14, 2005, we finally began transporting boxes of items from the museum in Centralia to the new building on Veterans Way. We started with the library books.

We started putting together the thirty new display cabinets downstairs. A local cabinet shop cut the parts. Rick Fisher's workload was too busy at the time, so he recommended another cabinetmaker who gave us a good deal. I designed the cabinets and he cut the parts. We assembled the cabinets downstairs in the main gallery and pushed them against the wall until we were ready to fill them. We now had a total of eighty-five display cabinets, seven feet tall, eight feet wide, and twenty inches deep.

The volunteer cabinetmakers signed the back of the final case on January 26, 2005. Everybody who helped build the cases signed the back—Larry Blake, Ed Weed, John Pedersen, Bill Logan, Art Williams, and me. I don't remember which case it was now.

I helped set the tile in the bathrooms. Being a cabinetmaker, I built and laminated all the counters for sinks in the lavatories. C.D. Nelson

Cabinetmakers from left John Pederson, Bill Logan, Ed Weed, and Lee Grimes. Not pictured were Art Williams and Larry Blake. All the workers signed the back of the last cabinet.

Commercial Fixtures donated the cabinets in the event center and the laminate countertops were laid by Stan Lupkes.

Next, in February 2005, we worked on installing the blocks for the Wall of Honor.

Petty Officer 2nd Class Joshua Hills, a young man from Centralia who was serving aboard the aircraft carrier USS Abraham Lincoln, secured a huge but slightly soiled flag from the ship's captain. President George W. Bush was going to land on the Abraham Lincoln and speak in front of the flag, which hung in the hangar bay of the Lincoln. But the captain said no president was going to speak in front of a soiled flag on his ship so he ordered it decommissioned, destroyed, and replaced with a new one.

"I had heard from another sailor that his department was ordered to dispose of the thirty-foot by sixty-foot flag," recalled Joshua Hills. "I

Joshua Hills describes how he obtained this large flag for the museum from the USS Abraham Lincoln *in this photo taken by* The Chronicle *in 2008.*

immediately went to them and asked what they would be doing with the flag. Their response almost brought me to tears. They told me it would be decommissioned and sent to a facility to be burned and disposed of. I asked the chief of that department if I could have it. He said it would take permission of the captain of the ship. So I put in a formal request to get the flag and to bring it to the museum. At that point, I didn't know Lee and was not sure if they would take it or had room, but I knew letting it go to the wayside was not an option. The captain was happy to see it go to a museum and gave me permission to take it. So I rounded up a few friends and we went to get her. We tried to fold it in the traditional way but the triangle was way too big and hard to carry as the ship's hatches were not as wide as regular doors. So we ended up with it folded more like a towel. It was about three feet by three feet and was not light; it took two of us to carry it to the locker I had. I took everything I owned out of my locker and we shoved that huge flag into my little locker. I mean shoved—we had to kick the door closed. But at that point, I knew the flag was secure until it could be delivered to the museum. I had to leave the ship for a family emergency, so I entrusted a close friend, Petty Officer

1st Class Glenn Young of Olympia, Washington, to watch over it and bring it down to Centralia when they got home from the Persian Gulf.

"The next time I saw the flag, it was already hung in the new building. It took my breath away and brought a tear to my eye. I knew we had done the right thing. Just telling this story makes me have goose bumps."

When we brought this huge thirty- by sixty-foot flag to the new building, we noticed how wrinkled it was after two years in storage. Before we could hang it, we needed to remove the wrinkles. We saw soiled marks on it, too, but we left them there. That's the reason we received it. We figured the ladies married to our veterans would know how to iron the flag, so we called up some of the wives.

"We've got a great big flag we need to iron," I said.

I never heard so many different excuses in my life—grandkids, doctor's appointments, meetings—every excuse you could think of I heard.

After making eight or ten calls, I got the point. So I started calling the guys and asked them to bring their wives' irons to the museum the next morning

"Sure, I'll be there," each one said.

The next day, twelve guys walked through the doors carrying irons. We had sixteen three- by eight-foot wooden tables that we put back-to-back, eight in a row, two deep. It created a sixty-four-foot-long ironing board.

We plugged in six of the irons and each person pressed a ten-foot section. We hadn't ironed many when—poof! We blew a fuse! We blew two circuits before we finally figured out how to accomplish our mission. After ironing each section, we folded it over and ironed the next stripe. We ironed one stripe at a time. It took three hours before we finished. We were really happy when we were done.

We enjoyed ourselves, laughing and joking while we ironed. But the women really let us down on that one!

We had devised a method to hang the flag from the ceiling, using one-by-eights with a three-quarter-inch groove in one board and a three-quarter piece of molding on the other. We sandwiched the flag between the two boards. The flag is ribbed on top so we figured we could suspend the weight by attaching it along the entire top. We designed a pulley system to mount it, with two eyebolts on each board. We suspended it by twelve points distributed evenly along the length of the sixty feet.

Using ropes threaded through the pulleys, with six people holding the flag and six pulling the ropes, we managed to lift it all in one piece.

We hung the flag on February 18, 2005.

We've seen many reactions to the huge American flag when first observed by visitors. Most are awestruck by its sheer size. But two instances really touched my heart. One day I was conducting a school tour for a class of probably ten-year-olds. When we arrived at the flag, I asked if they would like to recite The Pledge of Allegiance. The teachers immediately agreed and the children lined up, placed their hands over their hearts, and looked up at this flag that was nearly ten times their height. With eyes wide open, heads raised up and immense feeling, the words began to flow: "I pledge allegiance to the flag of the United States of America ..." My heart swelled with pride for these kids. I wished every veteran could have observed what happened that day. I believe it would have made them feel their military service was even more appreciated.

The second incident occurred one day when I happened to walk past a veteran who was standing in front of the flag. From his graying hair and approximate age, I surmised he was either a Korean War or Vietnam War veteran. He stood with tears running down his face. I asked him, "Are you all right?"

"Yes," he responded. "But every time I see a flag like this, I get very emotional. I served my country under this flag and am very proud of that." Then he asked me an unusual question: "May I wipe my tears on the flag?"

I responded, "Yes, sir, you have earned that right." He walked over to the corner of the flag and wiped the tears from his face. I have always called that moment "Tears on the Flag."

In February and March we finished the carpeting, base molding, trim, and final painting. The end was in sight.

After the building was completed, we turned our attention to furnishing it. That was going to be quite an expense. In addition to the front desk, we created room for three people to work up front—two in the administrative office and one for the director. We needed desks, chairs, and bookcases for the offices, tables for the library, file cabinets, and tables and lounge chairs for the USO area. We also needed conference tables for the meeting room, storage shelving for the archival room and other basic office furniture.

Then Bryon and Donna Loucks, who both had recently retired from Weyerhaeuser Co., contacted a person who managed the company's warehouse to see if they could donate any used furniture. The response came: Come up and get anything you want.

When we walked through their warehouse in Federal Way, Washington, we were flabbergasted by what we saw—row upon row of all kinds of furnishings and furniture—everything we needed!

We'd say we want one or two of these and the warehouse employee would ask whether we might want three or four. We didn't want to be greedy or wasteful. We took everything we thought we could use.

We ended up with three twenty-seven-foot U-Haul loads, a twenty-four-foot flatbed trailer, and a small U-Haul. I don't know how much it was worth—probably $60,000 to $100,000. Weyerhaeuser gave us quite a gift.

We did end up with extra chairs, which we donated to the Centralia Christian School.

These are all little miracles that happened. The odds of knowing that Weyerhaeuser had that furniture available and who to contact were slim, but the Loucks knew. That was remarkable.

The first letter arrived on March 4, 2005, delivered by carrier Jim Burk.

Loading the Stuart tank to take to its new home, above. Careful boys! One of the museum's fifty-five display cases moved.

In addition to the furniture, Weyerhaeuser has given us a couple of educational grants, including $10,000 to buy new computers.

First Choice Furniture donated the full-length heavy wooden tables for the upstairs conference room. Later, we invested in lightweight plastic tables, which are easier for volunteers to move.

The first letter to our new museum was delivered by mail carrier Jim Burk on March 4, 2005.

On March 5, we brought the old Stuart tank over from the old museum. It originally belonged to the National Guard Armory, which loaned it to the Lewis County Historical Museum. Bill Thompson of Bill's Hydraulics hauled the tank over to the museum, at no charge.

On March 20, we started moving the fifty-five display cases from Centralia to the new museum. It took us two days to move everything. We kept the items in the display cases when we moved them. We took all the photos off the walls, secured the mannequins so they wouldn't tip over, and hauled the cases in a cube van. That was an exciting two days.

We added thirty new cases, bringing the total to eighty-five.

Lee Grimes makes a wish while throwing a coin into the concrete mix at the flagpole site.

By that time, the old building looked like it did when we moved in, but in much better shape. It was a little bittersweet because our birth was there. The building held a lot of memories, so it was kind of sad to let it go. But we didn't have to pay rent anymore.

The last mannequin remaining at the old museum was that of a Marine—the last man out. The old museum officially closed March 31, 2005.

We kept pushing back the opening date. We initially hoped to open on Veterans Day 2004, to parallel the original opening seven years earlier. But we weren't ready.

Then we hoped to open on Memorial Day 2005. But we weren't ready. We considered postponing the opening to Veterans Day 2005, but when we started putting finishing touches on the museum in the early summer, we decided to open for the Fourth of July. We scheduled the grand opening for Saturday, July 2, 2005.

In April we installed the supports for a large eighty-foot flagpole.

To support the pole, we set a big metal steel culvert in the ground. We dug a great big pit and threw pennies, nickels, dimes and quarters into the bottom of the steel flagpole holder for "good luck." We put in the culvert and then poured the concrete. Everyone made a wish, probably hoping for a successful museum. The flagpole was to be added later.

Financially, we were still running at the end of the budget, but we always seemed to find enough to pay the bills.

On April 27, we held a board meeting and Lewis County Commissioner Dennis Hadaller presented the museum with a check for $118,000. The money was used to help the museum comply with the American Disabilities Act.

In early May, North Fork Construction paved the street, the land around the building, and the south parking lot. The sidewalks, steps, and handicap ramp were poured with Dennis Wolverton doing the finish work. It was remarkable when you looked at the museum how many little bits and pieces needed to be done. It was like putting a jigsaw puzzle together—one piece at a time.

We needed to water-seal the block wall outside because we wanted to put tiles on the Wall of Honor inside. We didn't want water to stain the tiles or erode them, causing them to fall. That took us a couple of days to spray the exterior walls with concrete sealer.

From cardboard to letters, quite a job! But they did it! The eagle came at the last.

The Veterans Memorial Museum with the eagle and the slogan "They shall not be forgotten."

June 11. It took nearly thirty people to clean the 170 panes of four- by six-foot glass in each display cabinet, inside and out. It's a lot of work, but it's also fun. We do that once a year and order pizzas to feed the volunteers.

Then, on June 17, we installed the big Veterans Memorial Museum sign with the golden eagle on the exterior wall. Pat Swanson, Dale Ingle, Bill Logan, and I together installed the sign, which was ordered through Awards West.

Each letter required a minimum of two screws drilled into the wall. We drew all the letters on cardboard first and taped it together to resemble the semicircular shape of the lettering in the sign. That way, we could determine where to drill the holes. We climbed ladders, taped the template to the wall, and drilled the holes. It worked like a dream. After we drilled the holes, we put up the sign one letter at a time.

This literally is a museum that volunteers built. That's what makes it so special. That's why we are successful.

My wife was right. I always said I wish I could get a grant for a couple of million dollars to hire somebody to build the museum. But Barb said, "No, you want everybody to be a part of it."

"You want all the people who donated their time to be in there. Each one of those then becomes a part of the building."

That's why I really do feel that when my time comes to leave, the museum will carry on. Everybody has such a vested interest in this place, not just me. I know they would never let it die.

Chapter Nine:

A Parade of Veterans and a Grand Opening

THE NIGHT BEFORE THE GRAND OPENING, most of the volunteers had finally gone home, but I needed to complete a few last-minute details before the museum's debut.

Dale Ingle, Pat Swanson, and I were finishing the last cases.

"Well, that's enough," Pat said. He left for home.

Dale went to check the back doors to make sure they were locked and I shut off the lights in the gallery. I was heading back to the front door when I felt God stopping me. I recognized the feeling. I knew it was God speaking. I felt his presence.

God told me to sit, so I sat on a chair set near the cabinets for visitors who needed to rest. I felt like God wanted me to sit and be still. We had worked three long years to build this museum. I spent long days here at this building, working alongside hundreds of volunteers. I felt exhausted.

"Look what we have done," God said. Not what I have done. Not what you have done. Look what "we" have done.

I began to cry. What I saw was so hard to explain. It was a gift, a revelation from God, who has revealed himself so many times.

As I sat there, a parade of veterans I had interviewed a decade earlier, volunteers who helped start the first museum, many who assisted with this museum, who died before our grand opening, one by one they walked past me. I could see their faces as they paraded by; they were saluting me—thirty or forty men who had given so much to their country, and to this museum. I saw Stan Price, Don Masterman, Norm Willard, and so many others. I saw them all. They didn't live long enough to join us for this momentous occasion. But God gave them a peek at what was going on down here.

I bawled uncontrollably, releasing pent-up emotions. We had come so far. My shoulders heaved as I cried loudly. Dale walked up and slipped his arm around my shoulder.

This parade of veterans was another gift from God. He has revealed himself so many times.

I slept very little that night, tossing and turning as I thought of these veterans, wondering whether I had forgotten anything, worrying whether anyone would show up for the grand opening, uncertain if the program might be too long ... or too short.

Grand Opening

Dawn arrived and I took a shower, praying that the day would go well and God would bless us. People started arriving at the museum by 8 a.m., although our first event—the dedication of the flagpole—was scheduled for 10 a.m. It started with a few cars turning onto Veterans Way, but by 9 a.m., a line of cars had formed in front of the museum all the way to Newaukum Avenue. By 9:30, the line snaked out of sight.

I thought about the 1989 baseball movie Field of Dreams, where a farmer portrayed by actor Kevin Costner hears a voice and obeys, plowing under his cornfield to build a baseball field where long-ago greats gather to play the game. After he built it, people came to watch the games.

As I saw the line of cars, I thought it resembled the end of the movie, with people driving from miles away to see the museum. Cars backed up on Interstate 5, both northbound and southbound. It was an incredible sight to see.

We figured about 2,000 people, many of them wearing military uniforms, gathered for our grand opening.

Rick Borovec represented the Twin Cities Sertoma and High Noon Sertoma Clubs from Centralia and Chehalis, which held fundraisers to pay for the $10,000 flagpole. He spoke a few words before a color guard of museum vets—one from each branch of the service—presented the flag. They marched in perfect unison, carrying the twenty- by thirty-foot flag, and presented it to the Sertoma Club.

I was so proud of them. The participants were Marine Staff Sgt. Harvey Rabbitt, Navy Chief Rick Rhubottom, Air Force Senior Master Sergeant Bill Peterson, Coast Guard Cmdr. Bill Schulte, and Army Staff Sgt. Bill Logan.

Retired veterans present a twenty- by thirty-foot American flag. From left, SSG Harvey Rabbitt, Chief Rick Rhubottom, SMSGT Bill Peterson, CMDR Bill Schulte, and SSG Bill Logan.

As the flag was being raised, U.S. Marine Corps trumpeter Mark Cecarelli played the national anthem. As the flag reached its peak, Johnny Dunnagan stepped forward to sing "God Bless America."

As he sang, I looked out over the audience and started to hear whispered words.

"Look up there."

"Do you see it?"

"Look at that."

I followed the direction they pointed. Two American bald eagles flew in from the south, directly toward the flagpole. They circled the flagpole two or three times before heading off in a westerly direction.

What could possibly have been more appropriate than our nation's symbol encircling the American flag as military veterans gathered below? It couldn't have been choreographed any better.

We all know who the choreographer was. I truly felt that God sent the two eagles to put his stamp of approval on the event. Every once in a while He will give us a sign that He's still with us and approves of what we're doing.

This was a symbol the public could observe. Even today, years later, we still have people commenting on that day when the eagles flew over the flag. It just touched the hearts of so many people here that day.

Next, we dedicated the Wall of Honor, which contained about 1,600 veterans' tiles, honoring veterans from the Revolutionary War to the present day.

A portion of the Wall of Honor.

Gen. Richard Read cut the ribbon to the wall area and spoke a few words. Then we dedicated the building. I was guest speaker for that part of the program.

When we opened the museum on Main Street in Centralia in 1997, I remember referencing Martin Luther King Jr. and his "I have a dream" speech. I repeated those words at this grand opening, only I noted that I never dreamed we'd have a 20,500-square-foot museum on two and a half acres to honor veterans. I dreamt only of a small museum to honor veterans, a small, peaceful place where they could sit, sip coffee, and reminisce.

The old museum had 1,100 members and thousands of visitors. Little did I know how much it would grow.

We all know God has a great plan for all of us, and by obeying his call, these things just naturally unfolded. I felt so humbled by the fact that I was actually a part of this.

I'm still frightened by that fact at times. Some people might question my use of that word. Why would you be frightened? I never was one who wanted to be in front of people. I liked to be part of the crowd. I was always a doer but never really a leader, at least in my own eyes.

We have a business to run now and we need to run it like a business or it will fail. We need to raise large amounts of money to keep it going. All these things frightened me, but I reminded myself that God is in control. He'll take care of all these things for us, but sometimes that's hard to grasp.

I felt frightened and grateful for all the people who had done so much to make this museum a reality.

The Nestebys sat on the podium with us during the ceremony, but they didn't want to receive any special recognition for their contributions.

I saw a sea of veterans in the audience and I knew this place would not be here if not for them. It wouldn't be here without their stories. It wouldn't be here without their sacrifice.

I recognized many people who had helped create the museum, including Mayor Bob Spahr, Mark Bolender, Dave Mundine, and volunteer contractor Dave Dralle.

I also publicly thanked my wife, Barb.

"When you've shared a dream and wanted to quit your job and go do something that has no income and no future, how many wives would say 'Go ahead and do it because God told you to do it'?"

Sometimes I wanted to give up and walk away, but I knew I

Heavenly Father
Great and wonderful God of all Creation,

We come here today expressing our thanks to you
for causing Lee and Barbara Grimes to have compassionate hearts
for remembering all U.S.A. veterans
of all wars and difficult periods in this great nation
while it struggled for existence.
We firmly believe you want America to remember and never forget
the sacrifices of these dedicated veterans
while holding powerful and evil forces at bay.

This memorial museum we see here
brings our minds and hearts racing back in time
so that we who live today can feel with great intensity
how they must have felt, as each man or woman donned their uniforms.
They were proud to fight for what they believed to be right,
as God gave them knowledge to know right.

Just as we are taught to remember
our wonderful Judeo-Christian God Jesus Christ,
so in a minor way, by and through this memorial museum,
we remember all veterans.
We walk in their shoes for a moment as we ponder their fate.
Help us Almighty God to never forget them.

And now Lord, we pray that each person who enters this beautiful building
and observes and meditates upon the contents herein,
will be renewed in their dedication of loyalty to our great republic.
We—each of us—ask your blessings upon this hallowed place
that you, O Lord, have caused to be in existence.

Once again we thank you
for giving to Lee and Barbara Grimes
great hearts of love for all veterans.

In the name of our great and wonderful savior
Jesus Christ,
Amen.

Dedication Prayer for the Veterans Museum at Chehalis, Washington
Lyle N. Kell 2005

Rev. Lyle N. Kell, former national chaplain of the Veterans of Foreign Wars, shared the prayer above at the dedication of the Veterans Memorial Museum.

couldn't do that. Doing something in faith is a funny thing. God gives some people a mission and they never question it. I question a lot of things. I do grow discouraged easily when things get tough.

Every single time that I became discouraged God sent someone to uplift me. Sometimes he'd send a fellow Christian to pray with me or offer words of encouragement. Every single time that I was down in the dumps, God sent someone to lift me back up.

Tears filled my eyes as I singled out Barb, thanking her for the constant support, as well as Loren and Patti Estep.

After my comments, the four of us co-founders cut the ribbon to the building. The total cost had amounted to $1,510,000 and we didn't owe a dime! God had provided through so many generous and giving supporters.

It was like a stampede as nearly two thousand people swarmed to the building, eager to see what it looked like inside.

Later in the afternoon, we held a separate ceremony inside the museum to dedicate the large American flag from the USS *Abraham Lincoln*, followed by a short concert performed by the Centralia Church of God choir. The singers stood on choir risers in front of the flag and Joshua Hills gave a synopsis of how the flag arrived in Centralia. He presented a Navy certificate giving the flag to the museum. Then I recited my poem, "Who Will Remember?"

That concluded our opening day ceremonies.

Shortly after the grand opening, Dave Dralle and his wife, Rita, flew to California for medical treatment by specialists after doctors discovered a cancerous boil on his back. It had started to weep. Dave had never said a thing about that during his time at the building.

I'll never forget the day he left.

"Lee, I don't know what is in store for me or if I will be back," he told me. "I just am so glad that God kept me alive long enough to help you build this place."

Dave, who never once said a discouraging word, survived the cancer treatment. He returned and continued to volunteer at the museum until about 2007, when his eyesight failed. He had undergone several cornea transplants, but his body tended to reject them. He's blind now, but he still visits the museum every week to kibitz and tells jokes with his fellow veterans and friends.

I am eternally indebted and grateful to Dave for all he has done. I thank Rita for sharing Dave with us and supporting him through the tough times. He was another one that God sent in our midst to help get this done. He had the expertise we needed.

Chapter Ten:

A Place to Remember

Running a Museum

When the museum opened, I remained as director and Patti Estep took over the administrative responsibilities as my assistant.

Museum volunteers Wayne Galvin, who had served in the Army Security Agency during the Korean War, and his wife, Charlotte, worked as unpaid assistants, developing brochures and informational sheets and helping with the bookkeeping. Charlotte volunteered as a tour guide for several years. We still receive support as a mission of the Centralia Community Church of God. We continued promoting the museum at fairs and in parades and we expanded our veterans' recognition programs.

About a thousand people visited the museum every month.

We honored our volunteers once a year with a picnic. We barbecue hamburgers and hot dogs for sixty to eighty people. It's amazing we have so many volunteers we can call on throughout the year. We have a great time and, in October 2005, we resurrected our Scandinavian roles in a skit featuring Hagar the Horrible (Dave Dralle), Sven Logangardsen (Bill Logan) and Ole Bjornsen (yours truly). We told Norwegian jokes and taught everyone how to do the chicken dance. Even Baptist Pastor Allen Hull joined in the chicken dance!

We continued to participate in the summer parades in local communities and the Christmas Parade in Chehalis.

Sven, Hagar and Ole doing "the chicken dance" at a volunteer picnic in 2005. The crowd then got into "the chicken dance."

A Place to Remember

But on December 19, 2005, we were asked to participate in a very sobering event—the funeral of twenty-two-year-old Marine Cpl. Joseph Bier, who was killed December 7, 2005, in Ar Ramadi, Iraq, by an improvised explosive device while conducting combat operations.

We knew Joe and his family very well. While Joe was still in high school, he and his brother, Dan, and their father, Wayne, visited the museum frequently. They loved the military history here. Joe especially liked to talk to some of the Marine Corps veterans such as Ron Harmon and Jack Williams. He seemed to absorb the stories he heard, especially about the history of the U.S. Marine Corps. When he graduated from high school, he immediately entered the Marine Corps. He re-enlisted shortly before he died.

Joe visited the museum to tell me he was joining the Marines to serve his country. He was very proud of that fact.

On the day of the funeral, the museum provided hundreds of handheld flags to supporters lining the streets. It was a small thing to do for someone who gave his life for our country. A lot of veterans and museum staff attended Joe's funeral.

Display cases at the far end of the museum pay tribute to the ultimate sacrifices paid by three local veterans in recent years—Joseph Bier, Navy Petty Officer 1st Class Regina Clark, and Bobby Lund. All three lost their lives while serving their country during the War on Terrorism.

Shortly before he was deployed to Iraq, Joe was at home planning a fishing trip when he said to his mother, Carol Bier, "Next year at this time, I might be fishing in the eternal realms." What a prophetic statement.

Joe belonged to a group of young Christian men who met in Iraq and he had asked his parents, Wayne and Carol, to send him some hymnals. They mailed him more than a half dozen.

After Joe's death, the Marines sent home his uniform, coveralls, and personal belongings, including a hymnal Joe used in prayer meetings and Bible studies. They gave us some of his belongings to display at the museum.

When I opened the hymnal, I asked the Lord to open the book to a page with special meaning. I opened the book to a hymn called "Why Should I Fear the Darkest Hour?"

Forty-three-year-old Regina Clark of Centralia worked at Fuller's Market before being deployed as a culinary specialist with the Naval Construction Region Detachment 30. She was temporarily assigned to a Marine Expeditionary Force, where she died June 23, 2005, when a vehicle-borne improvised explosive device struck her convoy in Fallujah, Iraq.

Army Special Operations Spc. Robert Lund of Chehalis, a twenty-four-year old aircraft armament system repairer in 160th Special Operations Aviation Company B, 1st Battalion, was a Night Stalker who died March 23, 2004, in an over-water training accident at Key West, Florida. He had served in the Middle East as part of Operation Iraqi Freedom from December 4, 2003, until March 12, 2004.

Another Chehalis casualty of the War in Iraq was Andrew Keeler, who had served as a sergeant in the U.S. Marine Corps in Iraq during 2003 and 2004. He returned in October 2004 as a civilian and private security guard. He was killed when his convoy was ambushed March 25, 2005. Though mortally wounded, he managed to drive his truck to safety, protecting the lives of three other guards with him.

"Old vets" enjoying a parade, Dale Ingle, U.S. Army, Roger Flinn, USMC, and Jack Williams, USMC.

First-place entry in the Tenino Parade in 2009 depicted military crosses, with Lee Grimes, left, and Dale Ingle. Ernie Graichen and Bill Logan rode on the M274 Mule in the 2009 Oregon Trail Days parade in Tenino, Washington.

If we didn't have the museum, there would be no one place where the public could come to remember and honor their sacrifices. It's sad and yet we feel a sense of comfort knowing that we've provided a place of remembrance for those who have given so much.

When I see the family and friends at the cases of the fallen, I just leave them alone. They're here for a purpose, not to have me bugging them.

How does a family deal with the loss of a son, daughter, or loved one? This can best be answered by the eulogy written and delivered by Wayne Bier at the service for his son, Joe.

JOSEPH PHILLIP BIER

Born 10-1-1983 Died 12-7-2005

Joe died while serving his country as a United States Marine in Ramadi, Iraq. Joe was a challenging child to raise because he was always trying to live to his potentials and occasionally beyond them.

He makes me ask myself, "What am I doing? What should I be doing? Am I fulfilling my God-given life?"

I spoke to his recruiter an hour ago and reminded him to live in joy and fullness. Few men live a life they love and die doing what they love among friends and brothers they love.

We have been overwhelmed by friends and family (made by Joe—our Marine family). We have much to be thankful for as Americans and parents, a family with two Marines (Joe's brother Dan is also in the Corps). We have been adopted by this fine community.

America, you owe so much to your service men and women. It is a small community with which we have been blest. Our nation would not exist without these fine people and the sacrifices they have made for us over the last couple of centuries.

I ask all of you to support our troops and their families left behind. These people live in your communities.

I ask that you all view life with joy and exuberance; live fully—thank God daily and look forward always.

Turn from evil and support our freedom and the well-being of our neighbors here, in Iraq and elsewhere. We are Americans and that is what we have done well and will continue to do so to the honor of our past and present citizens.

A story:

Joe Bier at home before his deployment to Iraq with his best friend "Indy." Below, Wayne Bier, Joe's father, stands beside his son's memorial display.

About five months ago Joe called and asked, "Should I re-enlist? My Gunny has papers!" I told him he should talk to God for guidance. I told Joe he should ask himself: Did he love what he was doing? Would he rather be selling produce at Safeway (my job for twenty-five years)?

Three days later he called back with great enthusiasm and said, "Dad—I love what I am doing."

In Ramadi, Iraq, on the 230th birthday celebration of the Marine Corps (it's a Marine thing), Joe was sworn in to his second enlistment—a wonderful and proud moment.

Gone to be with his maker, we wait the day when we too will be with our Lord and be reunited with our departed ones in the Lord.

Proud dad, Wayne Bier

Sometimes people don't have anyone who remembers their sacrifices, but we do.

I was in a secondhand store in Tenino, Washington, when I found some military medals for sale for two dollars apiece. As I paid for the medals, I asked why they were selling someone's medals.

The dealer explained that the medals belonged to Michael Morris Cady, an only child who was killed in action while serving with the Marines in Vietnam. When his mother died, the second-hand dealer bought the items from the estate, including the medals.

"Do you have a uniform?" I asked.

She thought she had it somewhere. I gave her a museum business card and asked her to give me a call if she ever found more items.

Nine months later, I received a call from her. She had found the uniform, as well as Michael's Cub Scout and high school letterman's jacket. I bought it all.

Research showed that Michael Morris Cady, who graduated from Mount Rainier High School in Des Moines, Washington, in 1966, had participated in band, journalism, and the debate team. He attended the John Knox Presbyterian Church and completed one year at the University of Washington before entering the Marine Corps July 12, 1967. He trained at San Diego and Camp Pendleton before shipping out to Vietnam in December with the 1st Battalion, 7th Marines in the 1st Marine Division.

He was killed in action February 15, 1968, at Quang Nam, Vietnam. He was only twenty.

I wanted to know how he died, so retired Army 1st Sgt. Bruce Longnecker, a museum volunteer, posted a query on military websites on the Internet, asking if anyone knew how Michael Cady had died.

We received a response from a man who asked me why I wanted to know. When I explained, he told me what happened. Michael was the point man on a patrol when he heard something and radioed back to his lieutenant, who instructed him to proceed forward. The enemy opened up with machine-gun fire, hitting his legs in the first blast. He bled to death on the battlefield before he could be evacuated.

Michael Cady's Cub Scout coat, letterman's jacket, and Marine uniform, along with his medals and the note, are proudly displayed in Case 62. The case pays tribute to the life of a military hero.

Without the museum, who would remember Michael Cady's sacrifice? Now, he will never be forgotten.

Chaplain Stan Baker, lieutenant colonel, USA (retired) conducts an induction ceremony (extension) for Sgt. Brian K. Hill.

VANDALISM

Early one morning in June 2006, I was awakened at home from my sleep to the sound of a phone call triggered by the museum's security monitoring system, indicating an intrusion at the museum.

At about 2 a.m., I rushed to the museum, just fifteen minutes from my home, and found police officers already there. They had arrived three minutes after the alarm sounded.

The officers prevented me from entering the building as they wanted to make sure it was safe. It turned out vandals picked up a rock from our retaining wall and heaved it through our front window, then entered the building and stole a donation jar and a bag of candy. The vandals couldn't access the locked main gallery, only the gift shop.

We had no way to tell how much money they took, but police did find fingerprints. They found the large glass water jug used as a donation jar broken on the railroad tracks. They assumed the culprits probably hid the jug when they rushed away, throwing it in the weeds.

Because of the alarm system and the quick response of the police, the culprits vanished. A K-9 unit immediately picked up the trail, which led police to a house three or four blocks away. The police pounded on the door

An adult who answered insisted nobody had left the home that night. Police had visited the home in the past, identifying it as a haven for drug traffickers, among other problems. The parents covered for their delinquent kids. In the old days it would have required a public apology and restitution by the kids or parents. Unfortunately, that seems to be gone today.

I never wanted to enclose the front of the building. We wanted to keep the Wall of Honor accessible to the public at all times. But because of the vandalism, in October 2006 we hired Industrial Fabrication of Centralia to install a security gate and fencing at a cost of $25,000.

Since then, the only problem we've experienced is kids driving up and down the parking lot and sidewalks on motorcycles and dirt bikes, doing wheelies and leaving black marks.

We experienced vandalism three or four times in the nearly eight years we were at the Centralia museum on Main Street. They caught the last batch of vandals there, a bunch of young guys from Tenino in their early twenties who were shooting out windows with pellet guns.

ACTIVITIES CONTINUE

On September 17, 2005, the first car event took place at the museum when a Ford T-bird group brought their cars to display in the parking area.

The museum also served as an induction center for the National Guard, which used to use the old Armory. When National Guard officials saw the big flag at the museum, they decided to hold future inductions at our museum. They wanted everyone inducted beneath that big flag. Retired Army Chaplain Stan Baker, a retired lieutenant colonel, presided over the inductions.

On May 11, 2006, we installed the large "Veterans Memorial Museum" lettering on the north side of the building. Ed Weed helped on the ground, while Dale Ingle and I installed the sign. It was rather precarious holding onto four- by eight-foot sheets twenty-five feet in the air on a high lift, attaching the letters ourselves to save a few hundred dollars.

One of our celebrity visitors in 2006 was "Jug" Brown, the last Little Beaver on the TV series "Red Ryder," adapted from the comic strip of the same name. Brown signed autographs at the museum.

Through the years, many celebrities—sports athletes, Hollywood actors, circus performers, country musicians, vocalists, and many others—have endorsed the Veterans Memorial Museum by sending their pictures with a personal sentiment and autograph. All of these photographs are framed and mounted on the wall in our USO coffee shop. We've had the pleasure of meeting several well-known entertainers in person—Lee Greenwood and The Bellamy Brothers.

Lee Greenwood was performing at the 2004 Southwest Washington Fair where we had our annual booth set up. Knowing Mr. Greenwood was an

Jug Brown (the last Little Beaver in Red Ryder) and Patti Estep in 2006.

From left above, Lee Grimes, Patti Estep, Lee Greenwood, Dale Ingle, and Loren Estep with a personal audience with Lee Greenwood in August 2004. Below, from left Howard Bellamy, Barb Grimes, David Bellamy, and Lee Grimes with guitar and plaque presented to the museum in 2004.

American patriot, we extended an invitation for him to take a personal tour through the museum. His response was positive, if time permitted. I remember the day was not a great fair day—the rain poured down all day as it can in Washington. Late in the afternoon, before his final performance, Mr. Greenwood's personal secretary came to our booth with a message that "Lee Greenwood regrets that he does not have the time for a personal tour but would like to have an audience with a few of the museum representatives." Loren and Patti Estep, Dale Ingle, and I were available so we made our way in the drenching rain to his tour bus. What a personable man he was, with no airs about him at all. He greeted each of us and talked to each one of us as an individual, asking questions about our lives and the museum. When he came to Loren Estep, they hit it off immediately when Lee Greenwood found out that Loren had served as a Merchant Marine, which his father had also done during WWII. After about twenty minutes, he excused himself to prepare for his performance but first autographed a picture for us to place on our wall at the museum.

A month later, we were attending a concert by country and western stars The Bellamy Brothers at the Napavine Amphitheatre in Navapine, Washington. The concert was dedicated to all who were serving in the military and all veterans who had served. During their intermission, on behalf of the Veterans Memorial Museum, Barb and I were presented with a red, white, and blue guitar donated by Security State Bank and the Napavine Amphitheatre. All active-duty personnel in the audience were asked to autograph the guitar face along with The Bellamy Brothers. A plaque was also presented to the museum to commemorate the event. Museum member Ernie Graichen built a beautiful glass-covered case for the guitar and it now hangs in the museum's USO.

We hosted a stopover for motorcycle runs and some of those benefited the museum. For the 9/11 Remembrance Run, sixty-five to eighty-five motorcyclists start in Vancouver, Washington, and travel north on Interstate 5 to Blaine, Washington, near the Canadian border. We are the first twenty-minute stop on that run. Veterans make up a good share of the riders and the numbers increase along the route. By the time they reach Blaine, the ride has drawn several hundred motorcyclists.

We held our last WWII dinner and dance May 20, 2006, at the National Guard Armory in Centralia. It was a wonderful setting with a band performing the sounds of swing. Trina Gardepie again catered the dinner for us. We set up the chairs, tables, and everything needed for the dinner.

It was then we realized that time had taken its toll on our WWII veterans. After dinner, most of them left for home, leaving only younger visitors to dance. So we decided at future events to simply hold a dinner without the dancing.

We also decided to combine it with Pearl Harbor Day. We have several WWII veterans who served at Pearl Harbor when the Japanese attacked, including Cy Simmons on the USS *Oklahoma*, Howard Gage on the USS *Nevada*, aviation mechanic Bill Furrer on Ford Island, and Vern Jacobsen, who served on the USS *California* and helped remove bodies from the USS *West Virginia*. Only Furrer and Gage survive at the time of this writing.

We also continued to participate in local parades and host our annual remembrance days.

VIETNAM VETERANS TRAVELING WALL

During June 20 through 24, 2007, in conjunction with the annual Vietnam Veterans Remembrance Day, the museum hosted the American Veterans Traveling Tribute.

It was the biggest event the museum has ever hosted, drawing more than 12,000 people during four days. It was quite a sight to see 150 motorcycles escorting the Wall from Rochester High School through Centralia to the museum in Chehalis.

The tribute features a 370-foot-long, 80 percent replica of the Vietnam Veterans Memorial Wall in Washington, D.C., listing the names of 58,453 people who died or went missing in Vietnam.

The tribute also features nine separate panels with dog tags marking the names of military men and women who died for our country since 1973—in Desert Storm, Saudi Arabia, Libya, Lebanon, El Salvador, Grenada, Panama, Somalia, and aboard the USS *Cole*. Two of those gold dog tags listed the names of Joseph P. Bier and Regina Clark, both from Centralia, who died in Iraq.

Another panel listed the names of all 2,948 civilians killed during the terrorist attack on our nation September 11, 2001.

Other memorials in the tribute recognized the thousands of military men and women who died in earlier wars—the Korean War, WWII and WWI, the Spanish-American War, the Civil War, the Mexican War, the War of 1812, and the Revolutionary War.

Among the speakers were Brig. Gen. Richard Read, a Vietnam veteran; Col. Bob Howard, an Alabama native who served five tours in Vietnam with the Green Berets and was awarded the Congressional Medal of Honor; and Pat Swanson, a local Army Vietnam veteran and museum volunteer.

"The American military did not lose a battle of any consequence," Howard said. After the peace accord, the North Vietnamese Communists violated the agreement by brutally invading and defeating South Vietnam. He contended that "The war was lost in Washington, D.C."

Pat Swanson filled in at the last minute as Sunday's closing speaker when Air Force pilot Captain Edward W. Leonard Jr. was forced to back out because of health problems. Leonard had been shot down over North Vietnam, captured, and tortured at the Hanoi Hilton for several years.

Col. Robert Howard, U.S. Army (retired), guest speaker at the Vietnam Veterans Era Remembrance Day in 2007.

Pat, a native of Centralia, Washington, served in Vietnam with the 1st Air Calvary Division where he intercepted and decoded enemy communications. He shared how hurt he was by the reception he received at the San Francisco International Airport when he returned home from the war. He noted that he and other Vietnam veterans fought for a noble cause—to halt the spread of communism in Southeast Asia. He also said, "Never again should politicians send young men into combat without a clear vision for victory and the intent to see the job through to the end."

Volunteers prepare the framework for Vietnam Traveling Wall in 2007, above, and below is the Vietnam Traveling Wall at dusk in June 2007.

Pat focused his presentation on the healing that the Vietnam Traveling Wall brings to those who have lost loved ones, those who have lost friends and comrades in arms, and those who suffered and endure survivor's remorse.

It took more than a year of planning to make this event happen. We contracted for the Traveling Wall to come, organized a motorcycle escort, found speakers for each of the four days, set up a prayer service for Sunday morning, and built wooden supports for the Wall replica. Many volunteers helped prepare for the event, but the results more than outweighed any of the efforts that went into presenting the traveling tribute.

Pat Swanson coined the theme for the Wall's visit, "To Heal and Honor." Boy, did it ever! We heard about so many healings, and I believe veterans felt honored when they were here.

Some of the people shared stories with me. Two Vietnam veterans were traveling from California to visit a Vietnam veteran buddy in Chehalis. They saw a billboard near Interstate 5's Exit 72 listing the dates of the visiting Vietnam Veterans Traveling Wall. They called their friend and said they'd pick him up in ten minutes to see the traveling wall. They stopped at the information tent, asking about which panel bore the name of a friend they lost in Vietnam.

They found the panel and as they were looking at the wall, another man stood beside them, staring at the same panel. The three veterans asked the man, "Do you have someone on the wall?" He responded, "Yes, my brother was killed in Vietnam."

It turned out his brother was the friend these men had known and they were with him when he died. Afterward, the four went to nearby Sowerby's restaurant, where they sat talking for eight hours. They told this man how his brother died; it was the first time anyone in the family met anyone who saw him die.

It was good therapy all around, a moment in time when paths crossed that might never have happened had the wall not been here.

I talked to retired Army Command Sergeant Major Ted Jackson of Shelton, Washington, who had served several tours in Vietnam. He loved the Army, but saw several buddies killed in Vietnam. He and his friends stayed in a camper, remaining all four days, helping to erect and dismantle the wall in the museum's parking lot and with event security.

The second day, Ted stopped me.

Above, CSM Ted Jackson, U.S. Army (retired), Vietnam veteran. Below, the pain never goes away.

"Lee, I'd just like to share something with you," he said. "I know six or seven guys on that wall, all killed at the same time.

"I have not crossed that yellow line to go find their names," he continued, pointing to a center line stripe on the black pavement. "I don't know if I can. It's just too hard."

"Ted, I understand your feelings," I said. "But you know, they're there waiting for you and when the time comes and they are calling, you will go."

I patted his shoulder and left.

The next morning, we gathered for a Sunday morning prayer service near the wall.

Later in the day, I bumped into Ted again. He was all smiles.

"I just have to share something with you," he said. "Today, I crossed the line. I didn't go down to the information tent to see where they were. I just crossed the line and walked up to the panel that they were on."

"See, they were calling you," I said. "I knew it would happen."

"I went to that little prayer service you had this morning," he told me. "It's been more than twenty years since I came close to a church ... so it's been a good day for me."

He laughed.

"My crazy doctor will really like to hear what happened today," he added. I knew he was suffering from Post-Traumatic Stress Disorder. He had told me his therapist thought the visit to the wall would be good for him.

Later in the summer, we featured the Traveling Tribute in photos on the wall of our award-winning booth at the Southwest Washington Fair in mid-August. I ran into another Vietnam War era veteran there and he shared how his visit to the wall changed his life.

"You know when you had that walk of honor, when all the veterans walked up in front of the colonel and the active duty guys," he said. "I have been a drinker most of my life, but when I was walking up there along with everybody else, something came over me—and it was like something left me. What it was is the desire for drink.

"I have not touched an alcoholic drink in two months. It was as if in that moment I was cured of my desire for alcohol."

I saw him nearly two years later and he was still sober.

"I hadn't realized what the Vietnam experience had created in me," he said. "But I was able to leave it there."

Every year during the annual Vietnam Veterans Remembrance Day, Pat Swanson adds a touch of humor to the event: He places Jane Fonda targets in the urinals of the men's bathroom! It's a very popular place!

Private Tour for Medal of Honor Recipients

During the wall's visit, I gave a private tour that Friday night to three Medal of Honor recipients, Vietnam veterans Robert Howard and Jim Kinsman and WWII veteran Robert Maxwell.

As we took the tour, Bryon Loucks, a dedicated museum volunteer, followed behind and someone walked ahead of us to keep this a private tour. If anyone wanted to speak with the medal recipients, Bryon or one of the other volunteers kept them away.

As we finished viewing a couple of rows of display cases, I recognized a young man who entered the museum, a fellow I had met at the bowling alley. Josh Hall was a nice young man who returned from the war in Iraq with Post-Traumatic Stress Disorder. A few weeks earlier, when I had given Josh a tour of the museum, he cried. He didn't want to leave.

"There's something special in here," he said, staying after closing time. I had mentioned that we would have three Medal of Honor recipients coming to the museum.

As Josh approached, Bryon told him that he couldn't join us because it was a private tour. But as we progressed on the tour, Josh followed behind, keeping his distance. We reached the very last case, the one focusing on the war in Iraq.

"Gentlemen, I'm going to ask for your apology," I said. "I promised not to introduce you to anyone. There is one person, though, I want you to meet. This fellow back here, Josh Hall, is one of today's warriors and I want to introduce you."

Josh, absolutely speechless, started to cry.

These three Medal of Honor recipients treated Josh with such respect, it was as if he had received the prestigious medal for valor. They thanked him for serving their country, for carrying the torch, and they wished him well. These men had been through so much; they respected those fighting for our country today.

I asked if they would mind having their photo taken with Josh and they agreed. Then they left.

Three Congressional Medal of Honor recipients at the Veterans Memorial Museum, from left, Robert L. Howard (Vietnam), Robert D. Maxwell (WWII), and Thomas J. Kinsman (Vietnam), in June 2007.

I was a bit worried about Josh. I walked outside and found him smoking a cigarette.

"How're you doing?" I asked.

"I'm so filled right now with different emotions," he said. "I've never seen the Vietnam wall before. I saw all those names—I've never seen so much sacrifice in one spot as I saw on that wall and then I went over to the dog tags."

The Traveling American Tribute, which included the Vietnam traveling wall, also featured several display cases with gold dog tags bearing the names of those who had died in the War on Terror.

"My former lieutenant's dog tag popped up," Josh continued. "I was feeling so down—it was one of the lowest points I've ever felt. Then I go into the museum and you introduced me to these three Medal of Honor recipients. I never felt higher in my life. To be honest, I don't know what I feel right now—so low and so high, but I'm okay."

I had the photos developed and gave him a copy at the bowling alley. He was so proud, showing the picture to everyone he could.

The citations and information on the men on the tour can be found on the Congressional Medal of Honor Society website (www.cmohs.org).

★ Colonel Robert L. Howard (then Sergeant First Class), U.S. Army, Vietnam

★ Technician 5th Grade Robert D. Maxwell, U.S. Army, WWII

★ Specialist 4th Class Thomas J. Kinsman (then Private First Class), U.S. Army, Vietnam—Lived in Onalaska, Washington

We've also been fortunate to have several other Medal of Honor recipients in our local area:

Private First Class Dexter J. Kerstetter, U.S. Army, WWII—Lived in Centralia, Washington

Hospital Apprentice First Class Robert E. Bush, U.S. Navy, WWII—Lived in South Bend, Washington

Signalman First Class Douglas A. Munro, U.S. Coast Guard, WWII—Lived in Yelm, Washington (The only Coast Guardsman to ever receive the Medal of Honor)

It was sad to see the wall dismantled and put back in the truck. Everybody had been touched spiritually during the four-day event.

A PLACE THAT CARES

In the fall of 2007, I was working in the back room and had asked a man who retired from the British military and his wife to help me understand the meaning of different British insignia from WWII.

After about fifteen minutes, Dale Ingle found me there.

"Lee, you've got to come out to the front!" he whispered. "There's a guy out there who's breaking down at every case and I don't know if he'll make it through the museum. He's just returned from Afghanistan."

I wrapped up everything in about ten minutes and walked into the gallery. I didn't see anyone at first, but then noticed a young man in a wheelchair. I introduced myself.

"I understand you just returned from Afghanistan," I said.

"Oh, no," he said. "That's my father. He was looking for you."

About that time, a gentleman in his forties walked around the gift shop corner. I introduced myself.

"I understand you just returned from Afghanistan," I said.

"Yes, I'm home on R&R. I'll be returning soon." He paused.

"I want to thank you for this place," he continued. He turned his head away from me, tears rolling down his cheeks. When he turned back, I held my arms out to him.

"Do you mind if a man who cares about you gives you a hug?"

He grabbed me and hugged me so hard; I can still feel his whiskers on my cheek. My own grandkids don't hug me that hard. He whispered in my ear. "I didn't think anybody cared. I didn't think anybody cared what we do over there."

We can thank our news media for that.

"Sir," I said. "When you go back, you tell all your buddies that there is a place that cares. We care about you and all those who are serving with you. Never forget that."

As he left, I walked with him to the door. He was still crying and Patti Estep handed him a box of tissues.

"I've never seen a place that cares so much as here," he said.

He left. I believe he returned to Afghanistan. At least he knows there is a place that cares.

I wonder how these men and women can continue to serve this country when they hear the news media malign them and their mission so much. What kind of pain does this cause the men and women who are wearing the uniform? The media and these protesters should be so ashamed of what they have done. They just don't realize the pain they're causing, or they don't care.

Farewell to a Faithful Friend

The fall of 2007 brought a difficult time for the family of museum volunteers as we said good-bye to one of the museum's founders, Patti Estep.

When we opened the new museum, Patti served as president of the board of directors. Later, she also became a full-time paid administrative assistant.

Patti was a joy to have around, always smiling and very complimentary. Everybody enjoyed Patti.

She was an Army brat who welcomed visitors to the museum and also greeted guests at the Bethel Assemblies of God Church. She and Loren, another museum co-founder and her husband of fifty years, had two children and four grandchildren. At one time she owned six collection agencies.

Patti had suffered from lung cancer in the past, but after chemotherapy and radiation treatments, she was in remission.

Then, in early 2007, doctors informed Patti that the cancer had returned, metastasizing from her lungs into her spinal column and then her brain. She died November 18, 2007.

I visited her on Sunday, three days before she passed away. She was always thinking of others and how she could help them and she said to me, "Tell everyone at the museum I'm sorry."

Sorry she couldn't finish the fabulous work she had started. Sorry she couldn't give even more to a project that is a jewel in Lewis County. Sorry she couldn't do more for the military veterans she admired.

Wayne Galvin, who has helped with the accounting throughout the years, stepped in as administrative assistant on an interim basis.

We were still reeling from her death in the fall of 2007, when we were hit with a double whammy.

Patti Estep, co-founder, "We all miss you, Patti."

Chapter Eleven:

Resurrection Follows Devastation

It Rained and Poured

In the fall of 2007, we held our annual Korean War Remembrance Day and Veterans Day events.

Then, on a cold and rainy Saturday, December 1, 2007, we pulled our float in the rain during the Chehalis Christmas Parade. We figured we'd start finalizing plans for the WWII dinner on Pearl Harbor Day 2007.

But Mother Nature intervened.

By Monday, December 3, 2007, record rainfall during a "pineapple express" storm swelled the Chehalis River, which crested ten feet over flood stage and caused $500 million in damage.

This wasn't the first time floodwaters had threatened the new museum. On January 10, 2006, floodwaters overflowed the banks of the Chehalis River and Dillenbaugh Creek, flooding the lowland areas surrounding the museum. Water backed up the museum's sewer system. But three weeks later, on January 31, floodwaters actually threatened the museum, flowing into the parking lot and reaching eight inches over the sidewalk. That's the first taste of what was to happen. Although the water receded quickly, simply washing off the pavement, we realized then that more extensive flooding could threaten the museum. The water was two feet away from entering the building and we had built three feet above the 1996 flood stage level.

Then, in November 2006, another flood occurred and the water crept even higher, but we still felt protected because we had built so high. Water reached eight inches higher than the January flood had, creeping up to the second step leading to the museum. That left another three or four steps before it reached the main floor.

"We're looking pretty good," I said. "Thank goodness we built her high enough."

We patted ourselves on the back, happy to find no damage, other than the need to spray mud from the parking lot.

On December 1, 2007, I experienced the cold blustering rain while waiting for the Christmas Parade to begin and listened to weather reports describing the heavy rain forecast for Sunday and Monday predicted to cause lowland rivers to flow over their banks. The rain kept falling, melting snow in the hills, gorging the Chehalis River, backing up Dillenbaugh Creek.

By Monday afternoon, I couldn't reach the museum, as police shut down Interstate 5 and many access roads, but I wasn't all that concerned. We had built three feet higher than the record 1996 flood levels and we had escaped flooding in 2006. I didn't expect the water to seep into the museum.

I saw an aerial photograph on television that showed the flooding. The helicopter was positioned directly over the museum and I could still see asphalt around the perimeter of the building.

The river had crested two hours before the photo was taken so the water had already receded somewhat. I thought we had dodged a bullet.

The water continued to recede Tuesday and, by Wednesday morning, Newaukum Avenue had opened up, so we were finally able to reach the building.

Dale Ingle, a board member and volunteer, called me to say he was going to try to reach the museum. Jim DeBruler, another volunteer, said he'd like to come along. The three of us met and drove in a truck as far as Veterans Way, which was still covered with water.

We pulled on our rubber hip waders, which were supposed to keep us dry as we sloshed through the muddy floodwaters to the museum. Little did I know, my old hip waders had holes, so my rubber boots were filled with water to the thigh by the time we reached the building.

I started to get a funny feeling as I saw debris on the steps and logs

Veterans Memorial Museum shortly after the crest of the December 2007 flood.

and pallets near the handrails. That didn't look good. It meant the water had reached higher than it appeared on the television.

We entered the shop area first, turned on the lights, and knew in an instant that water had filled the building. Brown muck covered everything in the shop, a moldy stench permeated the building and we saw items had floated off the floor.

We walked into the main gallery and our hearts fell. Nobody spoke.

Everything was covered with mud. Water splashed beneath our feet as we stepped onto the carpet. Water still filled most of the display cabinets, soaking precious letters, priceless photos, and irreplaceable historical artifacts.

What could we say? We just looked at each other and shook our heads.

We walked into the gift shop, where we saw merchandise racks tipped over, T-shirts, mugs, caps, and music CDs on the floor, soaked and muddied. Water washed much of the merchandise into the gallery gates, so we realized the water had flowed from south to north.

We peered into the library, where books washed off the shelves covered the floor, soggy and ruined. Books on the shelves swelled so tight we couldn't pull them out.

Water flowed beneath the desks in the offices, ruining our computer equipment, piling up brown mud against the furniture. I looked around and fell into my desk chair.

My mind clicked on all cylinders at once, seeing the brown water, damaged library books, soggy artifacts, ruined carpet, muddy display cases. It was too much, just too much.

After all our work, I couldn't help wondering, *Why did this have to happen so soon after we opened?* I knew many others were suffering even more because of the flood—a man in Winlock lost his life and dozens of others saw floodwaters destroy their homes and possessions.

For a minute, I sat there, asking, Why Lord? Why did this happen?

But I realized this is just part of life. God didn't send the flood; it was simply an act of nature. We could sit here and cry about it, or pull up our bootstraps, hit it head on, and take care of it. We've never backed away from anything.

I was actually overwhelmed by the amount of work that needed to be done. I felt lost as to what steps to take. I looked at the damage and then at Dale and Jim and realized we needed help.

I called the radio station and KELA put us directly on the air. At 10:30 a.m., during the radio interview, I described the damage to the museum and asked for helpers to begin cleaning up immediately.

By 1 p.m., thirty or forty people had waded through the water to help. Some were museum members, others complete strangers.

Before we did anything else, we walked through the museum to assess the damage.

We drilled two or three holes into the bottom of each display cabinet to let out the water.

And in the back room, where we stored items donated to the museum but not yet on display, we found that murky water had seeped into the boxes stored on the bottom of the tall metal storage racks, although the cardboard itself helped to filter out the silt. We needed to open those boxes and dry out everything soaked with water.

When people had started to show up, we put them to work cutting up the 12,000 square feet of carpeting that covered the gallery and gift shop, about the same amount used in six houses. We cut it into three-foot sections and hauled soggy pieces from the building. The softened carpet glue stuck to everything. And the soggy carpet sloshed over the cabinets as it was hauled out.

I called Superior Refuse, which brought in a huge Dumpster before the day ended. We dumped in the carpeting, debris, destroyed items.

As we worked, I spied my good friend, Mike Brower, whom I had worked with years earlier in a cabinet shop. He climbed on top of the display cabinets and disconnected the electrical hookups, pulling the chains of wire from the connection box. We didn't lose power and we didn't want anyone to be electrocuted.

That first day, we worked late into the evening hours, sucking water out with shop vacs, hauling bucket after bucket away from the building, dumping it outside where water still surrounded the museum.

By the end of the first day, we had done a tremendous amount of work. All the carpeting, except that beneath the cabinets and library shelves, had been hauled out of the building.

We started again early the next morning with about forty volunteers, pulling the display cabinets off the carpeting so we could remove it. We tossed about 20 percent of the books in our library that were too damaged or swollen beyond repair. The dry books—several thousand altogether—we packed in boxes and hauled upstairs to the event center.

We pulled apart the library shelving, yanked out the carpet beneath, and removed the file cabinets, sorting through the soggy papers in the bottom drawers, keeping important papers and tossing the rest. Water ruined the ink on most of the papers.

By the end of the second day, we had pulled everything and moved it upstairs.

On the main floor, we had removed all the carpet and washed the floors at least twice with bleach and disinfectants. We sucked up the chemicals and dirty water with shop vacuums. Finally, after the third washing, the floor looked clean, although water still seeped out from the concrete.

We were lucky in one respect. Normally our elevator is on the ground floor, but it was upstairs when the flood occurred, so it escaped damage. However, the elevator shaft itself was full of water.

The second night, George Gill Construction brought in a sump pump to suck out the water in the concrete elevator pit. We could see water running back in each of the three times they pumped out the water. It was as if cracks developed in the concrete. Finally, only two or three inches remained in the shaft.

We set up thirty or so eight-foot-long tables in the event center. Volunteers took everything from the bottom boxes in the accessions room and spread out the items to dry, keeping the names and numbers associated with them together.

Lee Grimes accepting cleaned VCR tapes and remastered DVDs of veterans' interviews from First Gentleman Mike Gregoire, a Vietnam veteran and husband of Washington Gov. Christine Gregoire, in February 2008.

On the third day, December 7, I was working in the accessions room, sifting through boxes, and discovered one containing all the oral history interviews I had conducted—the very heart of the museum, the seed that grew into this museum. I had stored them on an upper shelf in the room, but one of the volunteers had moved the box to the lower shelf and it was covered in mud.

As I lifted a VCR tape, water flowed out. Silt covered my hands. They're gone! That really hit me. I held this soggy box, realizing that I held about eighty lives and their stories and it really got to me. I cried for the first time through this ordeal.

About that time, in walked Washington's First Gentleman Mike Gregoire, a Vietnam veteran and husband to Gov. Christine Gregoire. He visited the museum three or four times during the cleanup.

"What's wrong, Lee?" he asked.

I told him about the tapes.

"Can I take them with me? I can check at the state to see if they can save them."

"Boy, if you could do that, what a blessing it would be!" I exclaimed.

He called three or four days later to say he found a place that could clean and remaster the tapes. After the work was completed, on February 7, 2008, Mike Gregoire presented the restored tapes to us. They all worked—that portion of our history was saved. They also placed the interviews on DVDs.

That, to me, was probably most important of all.

While some people worked upstairs, others tackled the main gallery.

We saw damage to many of our weapons, which is the largest weapons display on public exhibit on the West Coast. Silty mud encased many of the guns and others started to rust because of moisture in the air.

The first day, we put a call out for gunsmiths and two showed up. One brought his teenage children and they all started pulling the guns from the cases, one by one, and carefully cleaning each item. They worked in the back room using light steel wool to remove the rust, oiled the wood, and put the guns back together again. They completed the project in about a month and every piece looked good when they were finished.

Other gunsmiths arrived during the next month or so, helping to restore each gun, including those we had kept in storage.

Then we turned our attention to the artifacts.

Everything in the cabinets from a foot down was covered with brown silt, caustic enough to eat the finish off some of the furniture. We knew if it dried on the artifacts, we'd have trouble saving them. It stuck like glue. So we shoved all the cabinets to the west end of the main gallery, leaving up to 5,000 square feet of open space on the concrete floor still weeping moisture.

We brought in tarps and covered the floor, creating a barrier between the concrete and the open air.

We visited antique stores, secondhand shops, and the Goodwill to buy several Grandma-style clothes racks, which we opened up to hang the paper artifacts so they could dry. Another volunteer made several more of the racks. By the fourth day, we were ready to work on the artifacts.

We donned rubber gloves and used cleaning solutions, disinfectants, paper towels, toothbrushes, toothpicks, and brushes to clean each item. Although we bought masks, many people didn't use them and some developed respiratory problems because of the mold spores.

Volunteers arrived every day, most of them senior citizens who sat at tables and cleaned artifacts. We needed to make sure the accession number remained intact and we knew which cabinet it had been stored in. We made large numbers, one through eighty-five, which we placed on the tarps, and volunteers worked on one cabinet at a time. Some of the items did get mixed up, but I think we did very well in utter chaos.

As for the clothing on the mannequins in the cabinets, many people took those home for hand-washing or cleaning on a slow cycle in their washing machines. Some we took to the dry cleaners in town and none of those charged us a nickel.

It was just an amazing thing to watch these people come, day after day. They sat there and talked and laughed.

We turned the heat pumps up to 95 degrees and the fan on high to keep the air circulating. We opened the doors during the day to exhaust the damp air inside.

Mike Gregoire arranged to have a state archivist visit us to make sure we were cleaning and restoring the artifacts properly. Basically what we were doing was correct. Common sense is still pretty well the best method of doing things in all aspects of life.

State workers did take three or four older documents from the 1860s to restore using dehumidifiers, whereas we air-dried most of the other artifacts. We also had to weigh the cost of cleaning and restoring some artifacts against the actual value of the item.

As work continued on the artifacts, we faced the issue of reconstruction.

As with any flooding, we needed to tear into the walls and remove soggy insulation and Sheetrock. We received eleven inches of water in the building, but needed to cut the Sheetrock two feet high around the entire building to remove the insulation. The insulation on the exterior of the wall was coated up to eighteen inches high with mud. The insulation acted a bit as a filtering agent, keeping quite a bit of the mud from entering the building.

It took two weeks to remove all the insulation. We couldn't find commercial dehumidifiers, so we ran fans twenty-four hours a day to dry out the building.

Tom Cole arrived at the museum with a fumigator. With everything opened up, he sprayed throughout the building and inside the walls to kill the mold spores. He even misted in the air to help preserve the artifacts from mold.

The next day, when we entered the building, we could smell the difference: no more mustiness, but simply a pleasing fragrance in the air. He volunteered his service and his mother bought the chemicals he used.

Then we contacted Bob Knapp, a retired Air Force veteran who is one of the area's premier drywallers. He agreed to help us with the finishing work. We installed the insulation and screwed Sheetrock to the wall. Bob arrived with his equipment and expertise and within a week we had it all taped back together and textured again. He donated all his labor and we paid for the materials—but then he gave us a donation check for the same amount we paid him.

Next we repainted the walls on the entire main floor.

As we grappled with the flood's aftermath and cleanup, something struck me as rather ironic.

All three Seattle television stations arrived to cover the flooding and visited the museum to tell our story, but none of them showed up when invited to our grand opening two years earlier. It took a catastrophic natural disaster for us to receive coverage.

As I was preparing for one of the television interviews, I heard a tinkle followed by a crash, bang!

I rushed to the gallery to discover that the weight of the glass in one of our display cases had settled so much into the soaked baseboard that it pulled away from the case, crashing to the floor. We lost about six heavy four-by-six-foot glass panels. We removed all 164 remaining panels from the cases so we could replace the front board, floors, and runners in each of the eighty-five cabinets.

I contacted Architectural Woods of Tacoma, a company I had worked with years earlier as a cabinetmaker. The company sold us the materials at cost and delivered it to the Original Showcase shop owned by my old boss, Rick Fisher. With Rick's help and the use of his shop, we cut the material and banded it with white material to cover the raw edge, then milled them so they could be used as replacement parts.

It was laborious work but it took the six of us— Rick, four volunteers, and me—only about a week to replace all the parts in the cabinets.

As we prepared to work on the floor of the main gallery, we boxed up the items from the accessions room, which were dry, and hauled the artifacts from the display cases upstairs to dry.

We ordered tile in January through the Home Carpet Warehouse, which had originally provided the carpet. We received the eighteen pallets of tiles, grout, and mortar at a reduced cost. The material arrived January 17, 2008, and we set the first rows of tile the next day. Five weeks later, on February 21, we placed the last tile on the 12,000 square feet of floor.

The last floor tile of the 12,000 tiles laid by volunteers, from left, Lee Grimes, Dale Ingle, Jim DeBruler, Carl Johnson, and Darrell Gutsche.

Then we started putting together all the display cabinets. We re-aligned the cabinets and screwed them together again, hooked up the electrical conduits and made sure all the cases were clean. We discovered a few more problems, places where the side of the cabinets had swelled a bit, leaving a one-eighth to one-quarter-inch gap between the cabinets.

We also needed to screw through the face of the cabinets to attach the boards to the cabinet floors, so we decided to add a ten-inch oak base around the bottom and crown molding at the top, with strips of batten between the cabinets. It covered the damage and made the cabinets look wonderful.

Ernie Graichen, Pat Swanson, and I did most of that work.

As soon as the cabinets were ready, we began reassembling the displays. It gave us the opportunity to rotate some of the displays. We normally try to rotate 20 percent to 30 percent of our displays each year.

We designated April 26 as the day of our grand reopening. Five hundred people showed up and everyone who did seemed amazed by what they saw. Many had seen the devastation. Now the freshly painted building looked like it had never been hit by an ounce of water.

At the time, it seemed to take a long time, but looking back, we realize that work was completed in an exceptionally short time. That's a tribute to our volunteers.

What's to prevent damage from occurring again?

If we had enough help, we could pile a couple of thousand sandbags around the building but it's so huge and, with others preoccupied with their own flooding problems, that's unrealistic. We'd need a place to store the sandbags, which would eventually rot out, and we needed the sand.

In lieu of keeping water out of the building, we now have a flood plan in place.

At the next flood warnings, six to eight people volunteered to stay at the museum and watch the water. We have cots to sleep on, food, restrooms, and water. We can survive here three or four days or a week.

Before water enters the building, we will open the cabinets and set up tables downstairs, pull all the artifacts two feet and below from the cabinets and place them on the tables. We'll put computers and merchandise racks on the top of the tables. We don't store any books on the lower shelves in the library anymore.

We felt safe before; we don't anymore. We know we're vulnerable. We now have a plan in place.

We discussed building a berm around the area with sump pumps behind it, but there's no way we can do it. The only thing we do is make sure the artifacts are protected.

We no longer have carpet, only tile. Tile can be washed and disinfected. Sheetrock and insulation can be replaced.

We have installed concrete barriers around the building to help protect against flooding.

The flood cost us $75,000 in material damage. We received many donations. The good Lord provided once again, giving us just what we needed.

We sent a request to one thousand members, asking if they could donate fifty dollars each to help with our flood recovery. Within a few months, we received $62,000. Then the local Rotary Clubs held an auction that raised more than $12,000. Weyerhaeuser Co. gave us a $10,000 grant to buy new computers.

We lost five months of income and it's questionable whether we can ever recover that loss. But visitations are still strong with good summers and falls.

Overall, I would say we lost no more than 2 percent of the items in the cabinets that were wet, primarily photographs and paper documents. We kept most of the items, even though they are damaged, because they are historic, simply worse for wear now. It's like people, who are often a bit worse for wear. God's not going to throw us out because we're a little worn!

Most people who visit the museum can't see the damage to the artifacts. They can't even tell that anything was flooded.

When I look back at the flood, I realize there was a purpose. It brought everybody together again and even more people feel a part of this place.

Volunteers resurrected this museum, bringing it back to life. Too many people realized this museum was too good a thing to let it die.

Chapter Twelve:

Home to Healing Angels

IN APRIL 2008, BEFORE WE REOPENED after the flood, a soldier wearing fatigues came to the museum. I immediately introduced myself.

He told me he had been to Iraq twice and he was preparing for his third tour. He had watched television images showing the devastation to the museum from the flood, so he wanted to stop on the way from Fort Lewis to his home in Battle Ground, Washington.

I offered to give him a quick tour. Halfway through, I noticed that he limped.

"Were you injured in Iraq?" I asked.

"Yes, I received a round in the leg," he responded. "It left me with a limp."

As we continued the tour, he offered a bit more information.

"One of my good friends took a round in the chest, but he had a flak vest on," he said. "It didn't penetrate, but it bruised him and gave him a sore chest. He was lucky."

Then the man seemed anxious to leave.

"You need to take a quick peek at the section showing your war," I said.

He began looking at the memorabilia from Iraq and I saw a change come over him. I stood back by the door and watched as he reflected. A museum volunteer told me I was needed at the front desk. "No," I responded. "I can't go."

I heard this young soldier say, "And my best friend was killed."

I saw him wipe tears from his eyes. The volunteer, realizing what was happening, left. The soldier turned, crying heavily.

"Sergeant, are you okay?" I asked.

He shook his head and started walking out the door.

"Sergeant," I repeated, following him. "Are you okay?"

He kept walking, never acknowledging my words as he rushed past the museum volunteers.

As he reached the door, I hollered, "Sergeant! We love you."

He stopped, turned around, and looked at me. Still crying, he said, "Thank you." And he left.

These guys hurt so much.

Visitors began stopping by the museum again, but some days are still slow.

One such afternoon—it was Friday, June 13, 2008—I looked forward to the day ending so Barb and I could leave shortly after 5 p.m. for a long-awaited vacation to Minnesota.

Bill Logan and I were working at the museum, but the parking lot was empty. At 2 p.m., I told Bill that if it remained slow and nobody stopped by, we'd close at four.

By 4 p.m., we still hadn't seen any visitors and there was not a soul in the parking lot.

"Let's start shutting her down," I told Bill.

Then I glanced out the window to see a car driving into the parking lot. As the man and woman entered the museum with their three teenagers, I put on a smile and introduced myself. They were from California, on their way home after visiting a family gathering where relatives in Rochester, Washington, raved about the Veterans Memorial Museum and encouraged them to stop.

The woman asked if they could see her uncle's things, which included a German pilot's wings he had taken from a dead man in Sicily. I said, "Sure, I know exactly where they are at." I also mentioned that we were closing sharply at 5 p.m. to start on a long-awaited vacation.

As I shared the stories about artifacts in the display cases, my gaze kept returning to the woman's soft, lovely eyes. I saw something there that made it difficult to keep from looking at her. I believe she was a very Christian lady and the Lord shone through her eyes.

By 4:30 p.m., we had not even reached the end of the first row. I tried to speed it up, but by the time I reached the back wall with the quilt, it was already five o'clock so I thought, *What the heck!*

When we reached the Vietnam section, I said that sometimes people refer to the museum as a healing place because veterans have left their burdens behind after visiting.

By this time my curiosity got the best of me and I said, "I don't know where your Christian walk is but I am a Christian and the museum was founded on Christian principles."

She responded, "I am so glad to hear that; I am a Christian too! I noticed that there was a beautiful stained glass window over by the wall that looked like it came from a church but it has military insets. What is that?"

She gestured toward the stained glass with the military motif.

I explained that the Grand Army of the Republic, an organization formed to provide benefits, housing, and political power to Civil War veterans who fought for the Union, originally placed the window in the Methodist Church in Bremerton, Washington, in 1902. Sixty years later, the Methodists built a new church and sold the stained glass to the Community Church in Indianola, Washington, which cut it in two, making two separate smaller windows.

Forty years later, in 2002, vandals broke windows in the Indianola church, damaging some of the stained glass. Indianola church members, realizing its historical significance, sold the stained glass to the Sons of the Union Veterans of the Civil War, which worked with the Daughters of the Union Veterans of the Civil War and the Ladies of the Grand Army of the Republic to pay for refurbishing the glass.

Then Sons of the Union Veterans of the Civil War contacted the museum to see if we wanted the glass. Of course the answer was a resounding "Yes!"

They delivered it to the museum in 2005 and we installed it with back lighting after our big flood.

After I finished sharing the story, I glanced at the woman.

"Do you believe in angels?" she asked me.

A bit startled by the question, I answered affirmatively.

Daughters of the Grand Army of the Republic (GAR) stained glass windows, more than 100 years old.

"You have one here," she said, pointing toward the stars on the large American flag draped on the wall of the museum.

I followed her gaze as she explained to me that when she was forty-two, she died on a hospital bed. She watched her body on the bed as her spirit left. She saw the bright light that so many others with near-death experiences have reported but then heard a voice tell her: "It's not your time. You must go back." She re-entered her body, doctors resuscitated her, and when she awoke, she saw five angels in the room. She asked their names and heard their response: "We have no names, but we are known as Rod and Staff."

Finally Psalm 23, verse 4 made sense to me: "Even though I walk through the valley of the shadow of death, I fear no evil; for Thou art with me; Thy rod and Thy staff, they comfort me."

She said ever since that spiritual experience, she has been able to see angels.

"And I see the one that you have here," she said.

"What's it look like?" I asked.

"This is one of the largest angels I've ever seen," she said. "The head is by the blue stars and the gown flows down to the second red stripe from the bottom. It's probably twenty-five feet tall. Long and flowing hair curls up on the end. I see no gender in angels. This one has arms and wings. Not all have wings. This one has wings. I can't see the feet because the gown is hanging so low."

"Does it have eyes?" I asked.

"Yes."

"Is it looking at us?"

"Yes."

"Is it saying anything?"

"I can't hear anything," she said. "It doesn't have a mouth but they can speak and communicate."

"I've always believed in guardian angels," I told her. "There've been three times in my life when I could have died."

"I don't see this one as a guardian angel," she said. "This one has a look of peace and comfort."

"Would it be that look is one of healing?"

She nodded.

"Then I understand why it would be here—to help comfort and heal those in need."

As we continued the tour, I asked, "Is it still there?"

"Yes."

"Is it moving?"

"No," she said, adding, "Its eyes are following us still."

She said her husband wasn't a Christian, so he didn't believe in what she saw.

We had concluded our tour and were headed toward the front. As we walked past the stairwell to the event center, it was about 6:30 p.m. but still light.

She looked up the stairs. "What goes on upstairs?"

"That's where we hold events," I explained. "Why? Do you see another angel?"

"Yes, at the top of the stairs in the corner," she replied. "It's a smaller one with that same look."

She looked at me and asked, "What really goes on in that room?"

"We honor our veterans and we have healing there," I said. "Many have left burdens behind. People are grateful for what's been done."

She asked to see the rest of the room so we climbed the stairs. She looked around, pausing when she saw the photos on the wall in the small alcove by the elevator.

"What are those pictures about?" she asked.

I responded, "Those are the pictures of all of our board of directors, past and present. You see another angel, don't you?"

"Yes, it is in the corner by the photos and that one is speaking to me. It is saying that the board must always pray before the meetings and ask God for guidance."

"Ma'am, we do. We have since day one. We always open our meetings with a prayer, asking God to open our minds and hearts to what He wants us to do."

I looked at her again, and asked, "Are there more?"

"No," she said. "That's all I see.

"Do they stay here?"

"That I can't answer," she said. "I would only know if I came back at a later date and they were still here."

She said the only difference she saw in the angels was their size and the aura. Downstairs, the angel was large with a green aura, while the smaller angel at the top of the stairs had a red aura and the one by the pictures had a blue aura.

She thanked me for sharing with her. I thanked her for telling me about the angels. I truly believe it. It means a lot to me. This was a reaffirmation that God is still with us.

I left the museum at 7 p.m. for a two-week vacation and never once worried about the museum. I felt peace within me, similar to the peace I felt when the eagle flew past the flag during the fly-by at the grand opening three years earlier. I said to myself, *Who are you to worry when God loves this place so much He sends angels to guard it?*

Several months later, when I shared this story with Vietnam veteran Johnny Dunnagan, I saw tears water in his eyes. When I finished my story, Johnny asked, "Do you remember when I told you about the angels that had visited me?"

Probably ten years earlier, when I started interviewing veterans, I had recorded Johnny's story.

Johnny served from 1968 to 1969 in the Army's 4th Infantry Division in Vietnam, where he was a water specialist, sucking up dirty river water and filtering it before delivering it in tanks to the troops.

On his last night at home on furlough, Johnny was lying in his bed when six angels appeared before him, two on either side, one leaning over him at the head of the bed, and one at the foot of the bed. The one at the bed's foot was much taller than the others—so tall it seemed to stretch beyond the ceiling, yet it was fully visible. In each angel he saw long flowing hair, gowns, eyes but no mouths or noses and a golden aura surrounding them.

Speaking, the tall angel assured him that he needn't worry about Vietnam because they would be with him.

When he left for combat in Vietnam, Johnny didn't worry about dying because God's angels had promised their protection. He served his entire tour of duty without fear of death. In fact, he never even saw a dead body in Vietnam or fired his rifle.

Nearing the end of his tour of duty, at the airport terminal at Long Binh, waiting for his flight back to America, they came under attack from enemy rockets. Most of those in the open shelter took cover in the bunker to his left, but Johnny stood facing the runway without fear. He knew he wouldn't be hurt. The rockets stopped about 200 yards short of the shelter.

Specialist Johnny Dunnagan in Vietnam, 1968-69, above, and Johnny Dunnagan when he sang in front of the Vietnam Traveling Wall in 2007.

Johnny was happy to be reaffirmed that what he saw years earlier resembled so closely the angels at the museum. He sings patriotic songs at many of our programs and he wrote a beautiful song for veterans called "Standing Tall."

The following is Johnny Dunnagan's story about how he came to write "Standing Tall":

"I had been singing for programs at the Veterans Memorial Museum since it began and truly enjoyed it. The song I usually sang was 'A Hero for Today.' I thought that it would be nice to have another song to sing occasionally for a change. Then came September 11,

2001, and the catastrophe that startled our nation. I was scheduled to sing for another program in the aftermath of 9-11 and was concerned that some young men and women would be going off to fight and I wanted to be a support to all of them. After I finished singing my song, I made the comment that I planned to write a new song. Having never written a song before, it took me about a year and a half to finalize 'Standing Tall.' I intended to write the song to incorporate the Veterans Memorial Museum's motto—They shall not be forgotten—in some way. As I look back, this song that means so much to me would never have been written or sung were it not for the Miracle Museum, Lee Grimes, and Almighty God."

Standing Tall

One step forward with a raised right hand,
They take an oath to defend this land,
And our Constitution granting liberty;
They train and they'll fight to keep us free.
They're from every town and village
All across this land, willing to sacrifice and take a stand
For liberty and justice for one and all,
Oh they make us proud and they're standing tall.

Chorus

Standing tall, they're standing tall
Men and women of our armed forces serving one and all,
Whether here at home or across the sea,
These are the brave ones who keep us free.

Veterans of our armed forces all down through history
Have fought in many battles in the air on land and sea,
They fought to defend our country, they fought for liberty,
They have sacrificed to keep us free.
Some missing in action, some prisoners of war,
Many gave their lives on some distant foreign shore,
The message here today is to boldly stand and say,
They'll never be forgotten for sacrifices that they made.

Chorus

Standing tall, they're standing tall
Veterans of our armed forces who have fought for us all,
Their victories brought us liberty;
These are the brave ones who have kept us free

Standing tall, they're standing tall
Though fallen in battle, I can see behind the wall
The highest price they gave their all,
I can see them standing proudly behind the wall,
Oh they make us proud, and they're standing, they're standing tall.

—Copyright ©
Johnny Dunnagan

Another time, a visitor arrived late on a Saturday afternoon during the summer. The woman had the same look in her eyes and the husband was retired military. I shared the story about how the museum started and I told them about the angels.

"The moment I stepped inside that door, I felt something very special I've never felt before," the man told me.

I mentioned that sometimes I feel inadequate to do this work because I've never served in the military.

She told me that some people are born to achieve God's dreams.

"You were born to do this," she said.

I do feel this is my way of serving my country and the men and women who fought to preserve our freedoms.

A New Perspective on Vietnam

In the fall of 2008, we rented the upstairs room to a financial advisor who gave a seminar on estate preservation. He teaches people about wills and living trusts. His name is Don Skanchy and he and his wife live in Brinnon, Washington, near the Hood Canal on the Olympic Peninsula. I met him the morning of his seminar, surprised to discover he was of Asian descent and a true-blue Vietnamese. I listened to his program, impressed by the information and his knowledge of estate preservation, and spoke with him afterward.

Don with his dad and driver, above, in a picture taken at the Saigon zoo in 1967. Below, Don received his commission with his mom and wife pinning on his second lieutenant's bars.

Don told me he was born into a very poor family in South Vietnam. His parents originally came from North Vietnam, but migrated to Bam Me Thuot in the central highlands of South Vietnam in 1954 after the country was divided. His family lived in a twenty- by twenty-five-foot house with a dirt floor, mud walls, and a thatched roof that leaked like crazy when it rained. He was the oldest of six children living in this house with his parents and a grandmother. Because the family was so poor and the situation not a happy one, early one morning, Don decided to leave. He walked out of the little house with nothing except for a pair of shorts and a T-shirt. He was nine years old.

For the next four months, he lived on the streets and made his way to Saigon, the capital of South Vietnam at that time. He remembers well those hungry days when he had to beg for food and eat whatever he could scrounge up. Living on the streets was very difficult for a nine-year-old boy. During the day, he spent all his time looking for food. At night he struggled to find a safe and dry place to sleep.

One day Don was walking along the street, hungry and sick, when he ran into a policeman. After discovering that Don was living on the street, this kind policeman took him to a nearby orphanage, where he lived for four years. Then a miraculous thing happened to this young boy.

In 1967, an American serviceman named Robert Skanchy was serving a tour of duty in South Vietnam. He was thirty-seven years old—a single man with a great heart. He had adopted a little twelve-year-old girl and wanted to adopt a boy as well. So one day he visited the orphanage in Cho Lon, a province of Saigon. Out of about 200 children living in the orphanage, all boys ranging in age from eight to eighteen, he saw a scrawny little boy and felt love and compassion for him, so he chose him to adopt. Don said, "Here I was, the skinniest, scrawniest one of the bunch and he chose me to be his son. It was the luckiest day of my life."

After adopting these two children, Robert Skanchy called a longtime girlfriend, Sarah Ann Mobley, who at the time was a lawyer and senior advisor for the NBC Company in Burbank, California. He told her, "Honey, I've adopted two children and they need a mom. Will you marry me?" So when Don and his sister, Nancy, arrived in this country on February 29, 1968, they lived with their adopted grandmother who couldn't speak a word of Vietnamese, while Robert and

Ann planned their wedding. Ann gave up her career as an attorney to be a wife and a mother to two Vietnamese children who couldn't speak a word of English.

In 1971 when Don was about fifteen years old, his dad was called to go back to Vietnam for a second tour of duty. Don was very frightened and concerned for his dad and full of uncertainty. One day he was sitting on the back porch, missing his dad and crying when his mom walked out and asked why he was crying. He asked her, "If Dad doesn't come back from Vietnam, will you still love me?"

He remembers this special moment of his life when his mother pulled him to her and asked, "What do you think?" He said he didn't know. Then she looked him in the eyes and said, "Son, I'll love you no matter what because you are my son."

That was the moment Don gave his heart to his mother and felt the wonderful assurance of love from his adopted mom. Seven months later, his dad did return from Vietnam due to illness and thus was discharged from the military in 1974.

Don graduated from Utah State University and became an officer in the U.S. Army in field artillery. After eight years in the military, he left as a captain and has worked in his present profession as a certified estate planner for the last twenty-five years.

When I gave Don a tour of the museum, he said three things that struck me. He grew quiet when we reached the section on Vietnam, choosing his words carefully.

"I am so grateful to every American who came to Vietnam to help the Vietnamese to bring democracy to this little country of mine," he said. "But you know people must want democracy before they can have it and the government was so full of corruption and was not ready and willing to defend the freedom for the people."

That's all he said. We continued the tour before he spoke again. "You know I have been to thirty-seven different countries in the world and the only country I would ever want to live in is America. It's the greatest nation in the world with so much freedom and choice. We can choose whatever we want to be."

When he moved from Fort Sill, Oklahoma, to California to embark in his new career, he was unpacking boxes when he found his Army uniforms, including his Class A dress uniform and his old BDUs (battle dress uniform). He said, "I looked at those uniforms and just sat there and cried. I was so grateful to have had the opportunity to wear those uniforms and to serve my country." I grew teary-eyed listening to him.

Today Don is living the American dream. He has been married to his high school sweetheart, Kaylene, for thirty-five years and is the father of four children and grandfather of six. He attributes all of his success and happiness to two wonderful adopted parents and continues to carry on their legacy. Don had the opportunity to go back to Vietnam six years ago with his wife and four children and found his old orphanage, only to discover that he was the only boy ever adopted from that orphanage. He felt very humbled and also very sad for the other boys.

Visitors and Flood Prevention

After the devastating flood of 2007 and the recovery work in early 2008, we decided to skip participating in community parades and the Southwest Washington Fair during the summer that year.

We averaged about 1,500 people attending the museum each month, which is good for us. We held our recognition days, although we're revamping the format as more WWII veterans pass away.

Bernard "Buck" Langdon of Burlington, Washington, attended the WWII dinner in December 2008 and presented the museum with a rare flag signed by Hideki Tojo, an Imperial Japanese Army general and the nation's fortieth prime minister, and twenty-some members of his war cabinet.

Buck, a young Idaho farmer, served as a guard in the Army at Sugamo Prison near Tokyo, which housed Japanese war criminals. The American guards hid the flag in their coats and asked the prisoners to sign it. The signatures on the framed flag have faded through the years.

Buck, who became a dentist and worked at the University of Washington for twenty years, also donated a collection of artwork drawn by Japanese prisoners.

Flag Day

Although June 14, 2009, was Flag Day, most people celebrated it lightly or not at all. Many never even realized what day it was. A married couple, Ron David and Kathie Larson, visited the museum for the first time. Ron, a Vietnam veteran, mentioned to me that his mother was very patriotic and loved the American flag. He had a copy of his mother's story with him and asked if I wanted to read it. I read it as they toured through the museum and her story brought me to tears. This story was written in 1989, two years before Suria David's death.

SURIA'S STORY

Suria David has no patience with flag burners. To her, the American flag will ever hold a dear place in her heart. If it were not for that flag, she would not be alive today. Suria is eighty-four years old and America is her adopted country. She and her husband raised six sons and one daughter, five of the sons serving in the Armed Forces, three during World War II, one during the Korean War and one during the Vietnam War. Her husband George David (now deceased) was a veteran of World War I and served overseas for two years.

Suria David.

In the David household, patriotism for America was an ideal fostered and nourished by Suria and George. Their children were taught to ever appreciate the value of citizenship in what the Davids considered the greatest nation on the face of the earth. Suria's love and respect for the American flag had its beginning in a little, dusty corner of the world far removed from the shores of America, in the northwest corner of Persia, just a few miles away from the border of Russia. The year was 1914, Suria was eight years old, living in the village of Gulpashan with her grandparents. The village of Gulpashan was a refuge for the few Christians who lived among the Mohammedans, who comprised over 95 percent of the population of Persia. The Mohammedans hated the Christians who lived in their midst and determined to take the sternest measures in driving them out of the land.

It was early Monday morning when representatives of the local Mullah appeared at the village gates to collect taxes. When all the men, including Suria's grandfather, gathered in the village square to pay their taxes, the Christians were separated, then dragged to the nearby cemetery where they were shot to death. Word of the atrocity quickly spread throughout the village. Suria's grandmother, fearing the worst, commanded Suria and another young member of the family to immediately flee to the roof of the house, pull up the trap door and stay there till it was safe to leave. "I'm too old," Suria's grandmother told them. "They won't hurt me. Don't come down until I tell you. Whatever you do, don't make a sound!"

At various times throughout the night the Mohammedan thugs would return to the house looking for the girls. In their anger and frustration, they destroyed everything of value in the downstairs apartment, leaving the house in shambles. The two frightened girls lay motionless on the roof all night, not daring to make a sound. As morning came, news broke that Dr. (William) Miller, a Presbyterian missionary, was in the village square looking for Suria's family and other Christian women and girls of the village, to escort them to a safe refuge in the town of Urmia, a short distance away. Dr. Miller, astride a horse and holding a large American flag in his hand, commanded the women to walk closely behind him.

It wasn't long before the thugs were informed of the women's escape and rushed to head them off before they arrived at the Presbyterian mission in Urmia. Dr. Miller, seeing the approach of the thugs, dismounted and yelled to the women and the girls to gather to him and link their arms to his. With the American flag wrapped around his body, Dr. Miller faced the thugs bravely and told them, "In order to harm these women and girls, you must first kill me, but remember, if you do harm to me, you will also be desecrating the flag of the United States of America."

In those days, the American flag carried with it an authority that few cared to challenge. The thugs let them pass and Suria and the others made their way to the mission and remained there until it was safe to leave.

This then is the memory that a frightened eight-year-old carried with her throughout her lifetime. Suria David still possesses an undiminished love for her country and its flag. Though she is far removed from the scenes of her childhood, she will never forget the day her life was saved by a brave man holding high the flag of the United States of America!

After they finished touring the museum, Ron and Kathie stopped at the front desk, where they both immediately signed up to be volunteers and have been here, contributing their time and resources, since that day.

The Flood of 2009

When forecasters again predicted high water in early January 2009, we put our flood plans into action.

I spent the night at the museum with board members Dale Ingle, Carl Johnson, Stan Baker, Pete Slempa, and assistant director Chip Duncan, keeping an eye on the encroaching water. When it looked like the level would top the stairs, we moved all the items from the lower shelves onto tables in the gallery, to prevent the artifacts from being ruined.

The effort took us three hours and by the end we were all exhausted. We all slept on the museum's surplus Army cots. During the night, it must have been like sleeping in an Army barracks: snoring to various degrees, cots squeaking as the guys tried to get comfortable, the bathroom door opening and closing, the toilet flushing. It was actually rather comical when you thought about it.

I couldn't sleep, worrying about a repeat of the 2007 flood. Every half hour I would go outside and check the rise of the floodwaters. We had a long pole that we had marked with inches and feet to measure the water as it slowly continued to rise. Early in the morning, it reached the top step—and stopped. It was only eight inches shy of flowing into the museum. The high water stayed for about three hours before it began to recede. We had dodged another fateful flood!

In the early hours the next morning, the guys snapped a photograph of me leaning on the metal railing at the front entrance with a fishing pole in my hand. I had learned that no matter how bad the situation, you can always find lightness in the darkest hour.

We stayed at the museum three days, putting all the items back in the cases. After the floodwaters receded, we faced a massive cleanup of the parking lots and concrete walkways but that was a blessing compared with what it could have been.

A New Plan

In September 2008, the museum bought the corner lot at Newaukum and Veterans Way for $65,000. An anonymous donor contributed $25,000 toward the project. We floated a loan to cover the remaining cost.

The plan was to tear down the old house and convert that lot into a paved parking area, enabling us to turn the south parking lot, which faces the freeway, into an exhibit area for airplanes, tanks, and larger static displays. The visual effect from the freeway was expected to draw people into the museum. It was to be gated and fenced with barbed wire to prevent vandalism to the equipment.

During 2009, the old house was demolished and removed. The

In 2009, I spent the night praying and watching the rising water, which stopped only eight inches shy of entering the building. Fishing wasn't too good. I think the water was too muddy!

demolition was supervised by museum member and volunteer Jim Smiley. Jim had help from his son, Jay, and other family members and friends, but the primary demolition team was once again inmates from the Lewis County Jail. Jim has a great ability to work with the inmates. He also oversees the mowing of the grounds, again with the use of inmate labor.

In the fall of 2009, we received permits for a civil plan, earthmoving, and a storm-water system using the donated work of Todd Mason Engineering. Museum volunteers continued to clean all the debris from the lot and cleared the brush. In 2010 fill dirt was donated by various contractors. The construction and completion of the project would be under Chip Duncan's supervision after I retired.

I worked closely with Chip so he could step into the director's position when I left.

The day Patti Estep died I received a call from Chip. I had met Chip in 2004 at the old museum. He was a missionary in Hungary bringing the gospel and Christianity to the Hungarian military. It was a challenge because people who professed their Christian faith were disparaged, but he persisted for seven years, establishing a Christian fellowship within the military units. After seven years, he felt his job was complete there, and he asked if our museum planned to hire anybody, but we weren't. He told me he felt called by God to work in our museum and he kept in touch through the years.

When he called after Patti's death, I felt it was an affirmation from God that Chip was person we needed to hire.

He told me he had a feeling from the day he stepped into the old museum that God was preparing him to be part of this mission.

If he feels God's calling him to work here, that's great. He's an intelligent, strong Christian man with a heart for veterans, even though, like me, he never served in the military. His wife is a chemical engineer.

I offered him an administrative position in February 2008. He arrived July 2008.

I saw in Chip what we needed for someone to take my place. He possesses the ability to manage the museum and a good knowledge of military history. He will keep the museum on course while always keeping his eyes on God, who inspired us all to start this museum. As long as our eyes are on Him, the museum will be a success.

Most importantly, Chip has a warm heart for the veterans. That's the number one requirement.

When I retired, I wanted Chip to take over my job as director of the museum.

Chapter Thirteen:

All Good Things Must End

WHEN 2010 ARRIVED, I HAD DECIDED that I was going to retire at the end of the year. The year progressed as usual, continuing with our days to honor the veterans, tours, speaking engagements, and so on.

I had known Julie McDonald Zander for several years and she, being an author, encouraged me to write my memoirs of the museum and volunteered to help me produce a book. Once a week for several months, we sat in the event center and she typed notes on a computer as I related this story. We laughed and cried and had a great time working together. This book would not be here without Julie.

During the year, one of our board members stepped down and I was asked by the board of directors to fill the rest of the term for that position. I accepted and hope to be on the board for several years to come. It is a way I can keep close to the museum and have some input to its proceedings. The board is important to the museum's future. Board members will need to make sure they continue the mission we set out for the museum. We put God first, we honor our veterans, we always seek His advice, and we never back away from the premise that God started this museum.

It had been sixteen years since God planted a message in my mind that said, "No, don't let them forget. Go out and get their stories." We

From left, Stan Baker (president of the board of the directors), Chip Duncan (new executive director), and Lee Grimes (retiring executive director) on January 23, 2011.

had been through a lot with God's guidance: from a small rented space to a new 20,500-square-foot building; from 1,606 visitors the first year to more than 12,000 visitors a year after opening the new museum; we had met many new veterans and friends and felt a great loss in our hearts every time one of them passed away; our special days to honor our veterans grew and culminated with the Vietnam Traveling Wall's arrival in 2007; we weathered the devastation of a major flood; we saw angels and eagles.

When Friday, December 31, 2010, arrived it was a bittersweet day. I packed my office belongings and at 5 p.m. locked the doors for the final time. As I drove away from the museum, I experienced conflicting feelings: a sense of relief that my mission was done but at the same time a feeling of sorrow that it was my last day and that maybe I was letting the veterans down. Yes, I shed a few tears. But all things in life have a beginning and an end and, for me, the end had come; it was time to turn the reins over to a younger person with more energy and, with God's guidance, new ideas and new visions.

At our annual membership meeting January 23, 2011, I was greeted with a retirement party. I made a ceremonial switching of the director's coat with Chip, although with him standing six-foot-four and me being five-foot-ten, the jacket was a bit small! Board member Pat Swanson, with help from board member Dale Ingle, made a CD of pictures throughout the years from 1997 to 2010. What a beautiful memory to receive. Pat's wife, Sherry Swanson, presented Barbara and me with new embroidered jackets. Museum member and volunteer Ron David presented a plaque from the museum volunteers and Rob Hangartner presented a plaque from the Veterans of Foreign Wars District 12 Officers. Vietnam veteran Tom Kirkpatrick gave me a beautiful knife in appreciation for what personal help he had received at the museum. Board President Stan Baker's wife, Maureen, gave me a beautiful embroidered small pillow with the verse:

"For everything there is a season and a time for every matter under heaven. A time to weep and time to laugh, a time to mourn and a time to dance. A time to serve and a time to RETIRE."

Board member Bill Logan presented me with a white cowboy hat, stating that it had to be white to distinguish the good guys from the bad. I sincerely appreciate that he gave me a white hat! Board member Carl Johnson and his wife, Pari, presented me with a memory book. In December of the previous year, the museum had sent out a "Top Secret" notice of the celebration and encouraged all of our members to write a short story of what the museum and I had meant to them. It was so touching reading the cards written by so many people.

We received a letter from then-Governor Christine Gregoire thanking us for what we had done for the veterans and the museum. The final presentation came from the Washington National Guard. Master Sergeant Steven Saunders and Staff Sergeant Nicholas Lopez presented a letter from Brigadier General Bret Dougherty. The general announced that I was bestowed an honorary membership into the Washington Army National Guard. This was the fulfillment of a lifetime dream—Yes, dreams do come true! We received numerous cards and letters with gift certificates from so many faithful veterans and friends. Barb and I shed many tears that day, a day we shall never forget in our lifetime! Barb plans to retire from her work in the next couple of years and we hope to enjoy each other as we travel across this great nation.

While taking a group or an individual on a tour at the museum, whenever I discovered one or more were veterans, I would conclude my tour with the following thoughts. I can honestly say nearly every veteran who heard this shed a tear, family members shed tears, young people who understood the sacrifices shed tears.

The museum sees three virtues in every veteran—

Sacrifice—Every veteran has sacrificed something, from the 1.3 million who have died in military service to those who served during peacetime and never left the country. You all have sacrificed a part of your lives that can never be replaced.

Honor—The honor you have had of serving your country and the honor you now have to call yourself a veteran. "Veteran" is a sacred and honored word within the walls of the Veterans Memorial Museum.

Heritage—From generation to generation, millions of men and women have served to provide and preserve our freedom. America owes each of you a debt of gratitude that can never be repaid.

FREEDOM! Paid for by the men and women of the Armed Forces—God bless each and every one of you!

A lot of people have asked me over the years, "What are the future plans for the museum? How far are you going to take it?"

The answer is very simply— "Wherever God leads us!"

Lee and Barb Grimes during the retirement celebration January 23, 2011.

Veterans Memorial Museum

"They Shall Not Be Forgotten"

June 15, 2010

Museum Director
Lee T. Grimes
Admin. Assistant
Charles Duncan
Board of Directors
W. Stanley Baker, President
Dale Ingle, Sec'y/Treasurer
Carl Johnson, Board Member
Bill Logan, Board Member
Pete Slempa, Board Member
Pat Swanson, Board Member
Director Emeritus
Dr. Wayne Galvin
Leon Bowman

Dear Museum Member & Supporter:

As most of you know, in January of 1994, I received a spiritual visitation at 3:00 in the morning with a message saying, ***"No, do not let them forget, go out and get their stories"***. Knowing this referenced America's veterans, I have obeyed God's word and have dedicated the past 16 years of my life to that very vocation. With 16 years of God's guidance and vision, the Museum that you all have shared your support in, has flourished to the beautiful facility we have today.

As with all things in life, there is a beginning and an ending. I am today announcing publicly that on December 31, 2010, I will be retiring as the Executive Director of the Veterans Memorial Museum.

Your support of the Museum's mission has been primary in the success that we have been blest with and I ask that you will continue to support this mission. Knowing that a retirement day would eventually come, I have prayed that God would send us a replacement that understood the heart of the veteran, was compassionate to the emotional needs of the veteran, understood the mission of the Museum and had the business background to carry on the future goals and needs of the Museum.

Two years ago, that prayer was answered when Charles "Chip" Duncan arrived at the Museum. Mr. Duncan was hired as the Administrative Assistant and has been groomed for the past two years to undertake the duties of the Executive Director. He has answered all challenges and I am in 100% support of Chip to assume these responsibilities on January 1, 2011. The Board of Directors unanimously voted to accept Mr. Duncan into this position.

Retirement does not mean that I will be walking away from the Museum, never to be placing my foot within its doors again. Quite to the contrary, I will be very active in the proceedings of the Museum, and especially will place myself at the disposal of Mr. Duncan for any questions or concerns that may arise.

100 SW Veterans Way
Chehalis, Washington 98532
(360) 740-8875
Web Site: www.veteransmuseum.org
E-mail vmm@compprime.com

Pat Swanson
Board Member

Sincerely,

Lee T. Grimes
Founder & Executive Director

Director Emeritus
Dr. Wayne Galvin
Leon Bowman

100 SW Veterans Way
Chehalis, Washington 98532
(360) 740-8875
Web Site: www.veteransmuseum.org
E-mail vmm@compprime.com

Lee's letter announcing his retirement.

Appendices

Building Located—The Work Begins

Keys to the rented WarMur Electric building, located at 712 W. Main Street in Centralia, Washington, were received April 4, 1997. The building needed patching, repairing, painting and much remodeling. The old chimney was removed and the bathroom was remodeled. Floor tiles were removed from the front (future USO area) and replaced by carpeting. Cabinets for displays were built one by one. But first, many loads of garbage and old garage sale items left in the building by the previous tenants had to be hauled away. How did all of this get done...

Volunteers showed up when it was needed most.

SECTION A

Painting

Berg, Sharon	Dooly, Les	Grimes, Lee
Blake, Larry	Erickson, Allen	Grimes, Shannon
Blanchard, John	Grimes, Allen	Roberts, Arlene
Browning, Mike	Grimes, Barbara	Weed, Ed
Dean, Larry	Grimes, Jeffrey	Williams, Betty

Carpentry and Remodeling

Estep, Loren	Hanson, Norman	Weed, Ed
Grimes, Lee	Matthews, Frank	Wichert, Ken

Display Cabinets (quantity 60)

Arrington, Evan	Blanchard, John	Grimes, Shannon
Blake, Larry	Grimes, Lee	

Electrical

Gardner, Randy	Rollins, Ken
Grimes, Jeffrey	Willson, Al

Stenciling

Grimes, Shannon

BANNERS—DESIGN AND ASSEMBLY

Grimes, Barbara

GLASS CLEANING (CABINETS AND WINDOWS)

Blake, Larry
Carss, Amanda
Carss, Raquel
Carss, Teresa
Grimes, Allen
Grimes, Barb
Grimes, Patsy
Grimes, Shannon
Rohr, Jeff
Williams, Betty

SECTION B
GRANTS AND IN-KIND GIFTS

GRANTS

Ben Cheney Foundation	$7,500 Display Case Materials

PAINT

Stan and Joyce Price	Gift
Olympia Paint Co.	Gift
Fred Finn, Owner	

LUMBER

Architectural Woods Inc.	50 sheets of material donated
Tacoma, Washington	Special pricing on rest of order
	Mike Hathaway, Owner
	Rick Mauritzen, Sales

GLASS FOR DISPLAY CASES

A Glass Enterprise	Special pricing
Centralia, Washington	Keith Ivie, Sales

DELIVERY OF DISPLAY CABINETS FROM SHOP TO MUSEUM

Northwest Mobile Structures	Flatbed truck for delivery
Napavine, Washington	Dennis Larson

CABINET SHOP USE, RECEPTION COUNTER, FILE CABINET DONATED

Showcase Kitchens	Items listed above—donation
Chehalis, Washington	Rick Fisher, Owner

Computer

Jeffrey and Shannon Grimes	Office computer

Security Systems

Custom Security Systems	Discounted security system
Centralia, Washington	Gary Floyd, Sales
	Jean Waschgau, Sales

Banners

Josephine Mark	Material donation
Joyce Cornell	Material donation

Carpeting

Home Carpet Warehouse	Discounted carpet
Chehalis, Washington	Vigre Family
Lee and Barbara Grimes	Gift of carpet

Television, VCR, Amplifier and Emergency Lighting

Stan Price Memorial Fund	Provided in Loving Memory

Flagpole, Rigging, and Installation

Cy and Helen Simmons	Donated flagpole
Bill Wegley	Donated rigging for flagpole
Cy Simmons	Installation of flagpole
Morgan Harris	Installation of flagpole
Larry Blake	Installation of flagpole
Lee Grimes	Installation of flagpole

Donation of Flags

Cy Simmons	U. S. Flag
Harriet Clark	U. S. Flag
Marjorie Lloyd	Washington State Flag
Pearl Harbor Survivors Assoc.	Pearl Harbor Flag
American Legion Post #22	POW-MIA Flag
Chehalis, WA.	
Lee and Barbara Grimes	U. S. Military Flags

TWO FILE CABINETS

Lewis County Historical Museum Chehalis, Washington	Donated two file cabinets

COFFEE POTS

Stan and Joyce Price	Donated large coffee urn
Lew and Vivian Jacobs	Donated large coffee urn

LARGE WORLD MAP

Centralia High School Centralia, Washington	Donated large world map

LARGE U.S. ARMY CLOCK

Bruce Longnecker	Donated clock

BOOKS AND ARTIFACTS

A large amount of books and artifacts were either donated or placed on loan from many people. We were very thankful for all of their items that contributed to the variety and number of items for the museum visitors to view.

CHARTER MEMBERS

ORIGINAL CHARTER MEMBERS OF THE VETERANS MEMORIAL MUSEUM

A charter member of the Veterans Memorial Museum is a person that became a member on or before November 11, 1997, our Grand Opening Day. These members showed their faith in the museum project when it was only a dream and before it became a reality. There were 141 individual members and 14 business/organizational members.

INDIVIDUALS

Adkins, Lundy "John"
Althauser, Dorothy
Althauser, Robert
Amrine, Herbert
Anderson, Joe
Anderson, Rometta
Bates, Hoyt
Becker, Jack
Berg, Sharon
Blake, Beulah
Blake, Larry
Blanchard, John
Bussard, David
Bussard, Mary
Calkins, Gerald P.
Cardwell, Joe
Cardwell, Sharon
Carr, Dana
Clevenger, James
Cole, Margaret
Cornell, Duane
Cornell, Joyce
Corrie, Mildred
Dean, Larry
Denison, Al
Dick, James
Dickinson, Shirley
Dickinson, Ted
Dixon, Carrie
Dixon, Jerry
Dooly, Harriet
Dooly, Les
Duby, Dr. George D.
Duby, June
Erickson, Allen
Estep, Harry
Estep, Jodine
Estep, Loren
Estep, Patti
Fick, Sandra
Finley, Ed
Fisher, Rick
Fortsom, William
Fox, C. J.
Gallon, Donn
Gibson, Kay
Gillmore, Robert J.
Graham, Maria
Greenly, Harry
Greenly, Larry
Grimes, Allen
Grimes, Barbara
Grimes, Jeffrey
Grimes, Lee
Grimes, Patsy
Grimes, Shannon
Grimm, Charles M.
Hanson, Nancy
Hanson, Norman
Hanson, Roger
Harmon, Ron
Harrison, Robert E.
Hayes, James
Hendrick, David
Holmes, Garth H.
Hudson, Richard
Johnson, Enid
Johnson, Vivian
Johnson, Warren
Ingle, Dale
Ingle, Linda
Kell, Dottie

Kell, Lyle
Kelly, Albert
King, Anna
Kinsman, Thomas J.
Knoechel, Helen
Krein, Marilyn
LeRoy, Herb
LeRoy, Fran
Lloyd, Marjorie
Lloyd, Paul
Long, Donald
Long, Twila
Longnecker, Bruce
Lowery, Terry
Maher, Fran
Mark, Josephine
Mark, Laurence
McDougall, Robert
Miller, Ronald
Moon, Fred
Morgan, Charlene
Morgan, Joe
Mosier, John
Oman, Betty
O'Reilly, Charles
Patrick
Orf, Dennis
Parshall, Clifton
Petra, Jeannette
Petra, Jim
Pettit, Francis
Pettit, Helen
Price, Joyce
Price, Malee J.
Redinger, Ed
Regan, John
Reinhart, Margaret
Roberts, Arlene
Roberts, Donald
Roberts, D. Burke
Roberts, Muriel
Rollins, Ken
Rollins, Sue
Schabell, Elwood
Schindler, T. J.
Schultz, Clarence
Scott, Stanley Z.
Seeger, Eugene
Seeger, Ida
Sexsmith, James
Shepard, Ruby
Simmons, G. A. "Cy"
Simmons, Helen
Smiley, Tom
Smith, Mamie
Stefon, Bill
Stubbins, Ryan
Swanson, Pat
Swanson, Sherry
Venemon, Robert
Whitener, B. J.
Wigley, Robert
Wilber, Eugene
Wilber, Phylliss
Williams, Art
Williams, Betty
Williams, Patrick
Willard, Norman
(WWI)
Winterowd, Buck
Winterowd, Sylvia

Organizations and Businesses

American Legion Grant Hodge Post #17
Centralia, Washington
American Legion Post #22
Chehalis, Washington
American Legion Post #215
Morton, Washington
VFW Post #2200
Chehalis, Washington
VFW Post #8044
Oakville/Rochester, Washington
Ladies VFW Auxiliary Post #8044
Oakville/Rochester, Washington
Ladies VFW Auxiliary Post #3409
Winlock, Washington
George Pendarvis Auxiliary Post #5878
Tenino Washington
Lewis County DAV Chapter #29
Centralia, Washington
Daughters of the Pioneers of Washington, Chap. #9
Lewis County, Washington
Centralia High School Faculty
Centralia, Washington
Centralia Square Antique Mall
Centralia, Washington
Joe's Backhoe & Dozing (Joe Hangartner)
Centralia, Washington
Security State Bank
Chehalis, Washington

Legal

A deep debt of gratitude goes to Laurel Tiller, Tiller Law Firm, without whose guidance and expertise, the museum would not have been possible.

NEW BUILDING GROUNDBREAKING

NEW BUILDING GROUNDBREAKING BEGINS

The new site of the Veterans Memorial Museum was located at 100 SW Veterans Way (formerly Thomas Street) in Chehalis, Washington. The area was cleared of tons of brush and debris and the fill work began. It was like people were waiting for this to happen. The volunteers and donors came daily and never stopped until the project was done.

A volunteer time sheet was set up and everyone was asked to fill it out and place the number of hours they worked. Most of the volunteers did this but there were some that just wanted to help with no recognition. The names that follow are the ones who registered their time. Without their generous help, the museum would not have become a reality!

Name	Hours
Arrington, Evan	5
Badavinac, Jean	6
Ballard, Larry	4
Biers, Dale	3
Blake, Larry	296
Bolender, Mark	165
Brooks, Forest	24
Chalberg, Vernon	8
Champ, Doss	16
Cole, Juanita	6
Davis, Brad	2
Davis, Tyler	24
DeAbreu, Frank	210
Doyle, Casey	6
Dralle, David	2,067
Dralle, Rita	111
Drop, Gene	19
Erickson, Allen	71
Erickson, Janice	6
Ernest, Jay	9
Estep, Loren	1
Estes, Wayne	-
Evans, Claude	10
Ewings, Garth	2
Ferguson, Roy	13
Fisher, Rick	80
Foley, Ryan	6
Galvin, Charlotte	2
Galvin, Wayne	48
Gill, George	160
Gill, Rusty	16
Gillaspie, Jeffrey	4
Giordano, Albert	14
Graichen, Ernie	35
Grimes, Barbara	36
Grimes, Jeffrey	2
Grimes, Lee	2,573
Grimes, Shannon	5
Grindrod, Kevin	8
Gutsche, Darrell	123

Name	Hours
Hagen, Keith	6
Hall, Jay	47
Hangartner, Joe	18
Hanson, John	2
Hatten, Al	6
Hearn, Jeremy	9
Holmes, Garth	14
Ingle, Dale	420
Jacobson, Vern	1
Jensen, Finn	57
Johnson, Nancy	6
Landmark, Chet	10
Lewis Co. Sheriff's Inmate Program	2,250
Logan, Bill	182
Logan, Elmer	205
Loucks, Bryon	199
Loucks, Donna	124
Lupkes, Stan	7
Maden, Jim	4
Masterman, Carolyn	39
Masterman, Don	8
McCaleb, Donoven	-
McHarness, Jim	8
Metcalf, Myron	6
Miller, Monty	6
Monohan, Lee	58
Moran, Fred	50
Moran, Tim	73
Morken, Doreen	6
Norris, Jack	5
Pedersen, John	94
Pentecost, Jerry	133
Perkins, Frank	29
Pisauro, Dan	7
Poyns, Bud	8
Poyns, Lillian	6
Rabbitt, Harvey	6
Rector, Jake	14
Rhubottom, Rick	169
Rollins, Ken	14
Schabell, Woody	4
Schilling, Joey	18
Shields, Harry	4
Smiley, Jim	24
Swanson, Pat	53
Swanson, Sherry	10
Terrell, Bob	6
Terrell, Ginger	6
Thode, Bob	8
Thompson, Bill	20
Thompson, Jim	91
Thomsen, Tony	10
Thornburg, Bob	131
Trodahl, Jason	8
Victorson, Dave	6
Walker, Bobby	6
Watson, Ray	6
Weed, Ed	684
Weed, Lois	7
Whitaker, George	4
Williams, Art	112
Williams, Betty	6
Williams, Jack	2
Williams, Lynn	6
Wirta, Rick	-
Withers, Warren	8
Wood, Tom	9
Total hours	11,767

100% CLUB

The following are businesses that donated 100% of their products or services.

Advanced Drafting Services
Bill Warren Rentals
Brad Davis Construction
CD Nelson Commercial Fixtures, Inc.
Chet's Construction
Country Boy Dozing
Darigold, Inc
Fire Mountain Farms, Inc.
First Choice Furniture
Foresight Engineering
Four Seasons Farms
Fred & Tim Moran Plumbing
Geotech
Goebel's Septic Service
Hampton Lumber
Land Clearing Services
Lewis Co. Sheriff's Dept.
Mason Engineering
MP & E Co.
Northwest Fasteners, Inc
Original Showcase, Inc.
Pacific Mobile Leasing
Pfaff Architects
Security Door Fabricators
Wal-Mart, Inc.
WarMur Telephone Systems
Weyerhaeuser Co.

THE DISCOUNT CLUB

The following businesses discounted their products or services for the good of the museum.

A & C Flagpole Co.
A Glass Enterprise
Access Security, Inc.
Adventures in Landscaping
Alderbrook Quarry, Inc.
All Phase 2000, Inc.
Allen Acoustics, Inc.
Architectural Woods, Inc.
Awards West Printwares
Blakely & Hout, Inc.
Brown Road Quarry
Brundage-Bone Concrete Pumping
Cabinet Consultants
Cenex
Central Reddi-Mix, Inc.
Chehalis Rentals
Chehalis Sheet Metal
Chehalis Steel Co., Inc.
City of Chehalis
CLS Communications
Curb Master, Inc.
Custom Security Systems
Cutright Supply
DM Construction
Dulin Construction, Inc.
Elan Painting

ESCO Pacific Signs, Inc.
Familian Northwest
Ferguson Enterprises, Inc.
Folsom Tile Works
Garth Ewings Photography
Gemini Carpet Laying
George Gill Construction
Glacier Northwest
Grant's Towing
Home Carpet Warehouse
Home Depot
Industrial Fabrication, Inc.
Interstate Steel
Joe's Backhoe & Dozing
L & M Striping
Lewis Co. PUD
Lincoln Creek Lumber
Main Business Supplies
Martin Sand & Gravel
Mary Doelman, Grant Writer
Mudslingers, Inc.
Northfork Construction, Inc.
Otis Elevator Co.
Palmer Lumber Co.
Pittman & Son, Inc.
Powder Coating Technologies
Quality Rock Products, Inc.
Ridgeview Overhead Doors
Rochester Lumber, Inc.
Rodda Paint Co.
Sandrini Pre-Finishing
South Central Concrete, Inc.
Stan Lupkes Floors
Sterling Breen Crushing, Inc.
Taylor Construction, Inc.
The Daily Chronicle
The Metal Mill
Travers Electric, Inc.
Uhlmann Motors, Inc.
United Rentals Northwest, Inc.
Viking Automatic Sprinkler Co.
West Coast Metal Studs, Inc.

Financial Donors

There were literally hundreds of individuals, businesses and organizations that donated monetary funds to the museum to raise the nearly $1,500,000 that was needed to finance the construction of the new facility. To see such an outpouring of giving for this endeavor truly shows what people think of our veterans and their sacrifices for our freedom. The motto of the museum is "They Shall Not Be Forgotten" and this motto extends to each and every one of you who gave to see this project to the finish. God bless all of you!

2007 Flood Repair and Recovery

Listed on the following pages are the names of the many wonderful people who willingly stepped forward to volunteer their time, goods, and services or finances to aid in our Flood Repair and Restoration Project after the December 2007 flood. The names have been transcribed from the daily log-in sheets that were placed on the reception desk. If someone did not take the time to sign in, their name will not be on the list. For those who did sign in, we have done our best to make out the handwriting. Please excuse us if your name is misspelled or missing.

Labor, Goods, and Services Volunteers and Donors

Adams, Adam
Adamson, Tainy
Admidon, Scott
Admondson, Scott
Architectural Woods, Inc.
Averill, Jan

Baker, Maureen
Baker, Stan
Banks, Josephine
Barr, David
Bayne, Gail
Bouault, Lou
Bouault, Olive
Braze, Gary
Broostrom, Bob
Brower, Mike
Bruman, Mike
Bunder, Ken

Carlson, Micah
Carlson, Wendy
Carol's Design
Central Sales & Supply
City of Chehalis
Chehalis Rentals
Cheney, Pamela
Clark, Allen
Clark, Dennis
Clendon, Jim
Closner, Leo
Coakley, Alice
Cole, Juanita
Cole, Tom
Cole, Tom Jr.
Conradi, Ernie
Conradi, Marliene
Cook, Charles
Crary, Royce
Cummings, Floyd

DeBruler, Jim
Dickason, Ernie
Dobbins, Cassie
Donyes, Robert
Dunkle, Jim

Erickson, Allen
Erickson, Janice
Erickson, Mark
Evans, Claude

Figueroa, Lindsey
First Choice Furniture
Fisher, Rick
Ford, Gayle

Galvin, Charlotte
Galvin, Wayne
George Gill Construction
Governor's Veterans Affairs Advisory Committee
Graichen, Ernie
Grimes, Barbara
Grimes, Jeffrey
Grimes, Lee
Gutsche, Darrell

Haas, Linda
Harmon, Ron
Harris, Tony
Hayes, Jim
Hogan, Pat

Hogan, P.J.
Holmes, Daniel
Holmes, Mary
Holt, Darrell
Home Carpet Warehouse
Hopkins, Richard
Horton, John
Horton, Paulene
Hutto, Stan

Ingle, Dale
Ingle, Linda

Jackson, David
Jackson, Jeremy
Jackson, Jonathan
Jackson, Ted
Johnson, Carl
Johnson, Pari
Johnson, Sam
Justice, Paul

Kehr, Steve
Kennenburg, Matt
Kililech, Dick
Knapp, Bob

Lacey, Jonelle
Larson, Dennis
Lewis County Chemical
Lies, SSG Shane
Lowery, Terry
Loucks, Bryon
Loucks, Donna

Macdonald, John
Martin, Andrew
Martinez, Adam
Mason, Bill
Masterman, Carolyn
Miller, Monty
Moon, Fred
Monahan, Lee
Morales, Maleea
Moran Brothers Plumbing
Mudder, Bob
Murchinson, George

Nelson, Josh
Nishiyama, Nissa

Original Showcase, Inc.
Ortez, Noi

Peterson, William
Powell, Ron
Poyns, Bud
Poyns, Lillian
Persle, April
Persle, Devon
Persle, Steve
Persle, Wayne

Rayland, April
Rayland, Devon
Ranson, Randy
Rasmussen, Al
Rhubottom, Rick
Rohring, Levi
Rosbach, Karl
Roses, Jim
Roses, Margie

Schilling, Joey
Schmidt, Dave
Sherman, Kenny
Shirer, Bob
Sisson, Becky
Slempa, Linda
Slempa, Pete
Smiley, Jay
Smiley, Jim
Stephenson, Lani
Sturdevant, Bob
Sundercock, Cody
Sundercock, Ian
Superior Refuse
Swanson, Pat
Swanson, Sherry

Terrell, Bob
Terrell, Ginger
Thompson, Ben
Thompson, Bob
Thompson, Ron
Travers Electric (Jason Wilson)
Tyler, Dan

United Rentals

Vervalen, John

WA State Emblem Fund
Wells, Diane
Watson, SFC Ryan
Watson, Sara
Weed, Ed
Wharton, Gary
Whitnell, W.L.
Wilkinson, Lerow
Williams, Art
Williams, Buzz

Williams, Jack
Williams, Lynn
Williams, Marilyn
Wisner, Dan
Wisner, Krista
Wisner, Tyler
Wojnar, Tom
Workman, K.
Young, Ryan

FINANCIAL DONORS

The museum records indicate that more than 533 individuals, organizations and businesses from all across America made financial donations to help with the recovery of the museum. This does not include the number of people who just dropped money in our donation boxes around the museum. The total raised equaled $68,184!

Without the generous people who donated their time, services, goods, and money, the museum would not have risen from the devastation of the 2007 flood.

God bless all of you who saw the Veterans Memorial Museum as a needed and worthwhile cause to honor the sacrifices and service of America's military veterans!

Board of Directors 1996–2014

Listed below are the past and present members of the Veterans Memorial Museum Board of Directors. Each member has brought to the board valuable expertise from their lifelong endeavors. The time and expertise they have shared with the museum has been extremely valuable and the museum is forever in debt to each member for their insight and guidance. Their recommendations have always been for the good of the museum. With God's guidance, they have kept the museum moving forward and always placed the service of our veterans as the primary reason the Museum exists.

Loren J. Estep
Museum Co-Founder
Board Member 1996–1998
Vice President 1996–1998

Lee T. Grimes
Museum Co-Founder
Board Member 1996–1998;
2010–2014
President 1996–1998
Treasurer 2011–2014

Leslie E. Dooly
Board Member 1996–1998

Bruce R. Longnecker
Board Member 1998–2000
Secretary/Treasurer 1999–2000

Leon L. Bowman
Board Member 1999–2007
Director Emeritus

Patti L. Estep
Museum Co-Founder
Board Member 1996–1997;
1999–2007
President 1999–2007

Jeffrey G. Grimes
Board Member 1996–1998
Secretary/Treasurer 1996–1998

George A. "Cy" Simmons
Board Member 1998–2004
Vice President 1999–2004
Director Emeritus

Kenneth L. Rollins
Board Member 1998–2000

Dr. Wayne W. Galvin
Board Member 1999–2007
Treasurer 2003–2004
Director Emeritus

Wade S. Samuelson
Board Member 2000–2005

Dale E. Ingle
Board Member 2002–2004; 2005–2014
Vice President 2005–2006
Secretary/Treasurer 2008–2010
Secretary 2011–2014

Patrick A. Swanson
Board Member 2005–2011
Vice President 2011

John E. Hanson
Board Member 2007–2009

Peter P. Slempa
Board Member 2008–2014

Carl R. Johnson
Board Member 2010–2014
Vice President 2010

Barbara J. Grimes
Museum Co-Founder
Board Member 2001–2004
Secretary/Treasurer 2001–2002
Secretary 2003–2004

Ernest A. Graichen
Board Member 2004–2009
Secretary/Treasurer 2005–2007
President 2008–2009

W. Stanley Baker
Board Member 2006–2014
Vice President 2007–2009
President 2010–2014

William A. Logan
Board Member 2008–2014
Vice President 2012–2014

Darrell R. Holt
Board Member 2012–2014